Guide

Tarragona Cathedral

Text **Antonio Pedro Martínez Subías** Photography **Jordi Puig**

Index

TRIANGLE BOOKS

Tarragona Cathedral

Introduction

The Metropolitan Primate Cathedral and Holy Church of Tarragona, dedicated to Saint Thecla, houses the seat of the city's bishop and has been thus designated as a sign of his pastoral ministry and the unity of believers in a single faith. It is also the mother church of the diocese, the centre of the liturgical life of the diocesan community, and one of Catalonia's most outstanding Gothic landmarks. The cathedral's sturdy architecture, monumental scale, austere elegance and rich ornamentation make it a truly unique compendium of styles with artworks that reflect the excellence of this iconic place of worship.

The cathedral complex stands on the highest point in the city on a site first occupied by a Roman garrison (218 BC). The city of Tarraco was built here and eventually became the capital of *Hispania Citerior* (27 BC). Its population is thought to have converted to Christianity during the 1st century AD, although no evidence of Christian art from the middle of the 3rd to the second half of the 4th centuries survives. The first references to the church date from the year 259 AD, and are found in the *Passio Fructuosi*, one of the *Acts of the Martyrs* that describes the martyrdom of the bishop Saint Fructuosus and his deacons Augurius and Eulogius. It was read in African churches, mentioned by Saint Augustine, and set to verse by the poet Aurelius Clemens Prudentius in his *Peristephanon* or *Crowns of Martyrdom*. These poems had a great impact on the Christian literature of the late Roman era and bear witness to the existence of a large Christian community. They also provide documentary evidence that the church in Tarraco had become sufficiently well established by the 3rd century. Tarraco reached the height of its ecclesiastical powers during the 4th and 5th centuries. When the city came under the rule of King Euric (476 AD) it lost its capital city status and became part of the Visigothic kingdom of Toulouse, and, subsequently, Barcelona and Toledo.

The cathedral complex stands on the highest point in the city on a site first occupied by a Roman garrison

After this period, the Roman architectural ensemble, which probably included structures from the large chamber used as place of worship during Roman rule, was converted into bishops' quarters and became the seat of the basilica, or *Ecclesia mater.* No traces of the building survive as it was demolished during the Muslim invasion which some authors date between 713 and 716 AD. The diocese remained vacant until Pope Urban II issued a papal bull, *Inter primas Hispaniarum* (1091), appointing the bishop of Vic, Berenguer Sunifred de Lluçà, archbishop of Tarragona, thus reinstating the episcopal see and starting the process of repopulating the city and the region known as the Camp de Tarragona. The fact that Berenguer was a peripatetic bishop led Rome to appoint Bernard de Tort to the post in 1154 on the undertaking that he would take up permanent residence at the church. The prelate came from the abbey of Saint-Ruf d'Avignon and instated the Chapter of the Basilica and Cathedral of Tarragona made up of a small group of clerics. He drew up the rules to be followed by the new canons of the order of Saint Augustine, through the *Quoniam in primitiva Ecclesia* constitution signed on 30th October 1154 and endorsed by the count of Barcelona, Ramon Berenguer IV.

The walls of the north-western and north-eastern wings of the cloisters are part of the corner of the façade of the imposing agora whose walls, built with solid ashlars, include a large portal and several blind windows. The fact that the cathedral had to adapt to the shape of this area explains the unconventional aspect of the chancel, which is south-west-north-east facing rather that east-west facing. The cemetery was placed around the eastern end of the cathedral and Archbishop Hug de Cervelló (1163-1171) built the hospital and episcopal orphanage opposite the outer wall of the transept in 1171. The lower tier of the arches survives today.

→
Buttresses on the façade

General view of the cathedral

Genesis of the building

Following the reconquest and repopulation of the city, Olegarius (1118-1137) was invested as archbishop of Tarragona. He deemed it necessary to build a cathedral worthy of the metropolitan primatial see. The scant, and patchy, documentation about the start of building work and its progress means we are unable to establish an accurate timeline. We do know that it was a long, costly and intermittent process.

The cathedral can be classified stylistically as proto-Gothic and was initially associated with the Romanesque style. It was begun in 1171 when the prelate Hug de Cervelló bequeathed most of his goods in his will to pay for building work on the cathedral and the canons' quarters. The usual process was followed: the chancel, the transept, and the naves nearest the façade enclosed by three doors and a large rose window. The exterior of the chancel followed the late-Romanesque style, made evident in the central apse resembling a military fortress with five machicolations, splayed loopholes, a central window featuring white marble archivolts and unfinished quadrangular towers flanking the main apse and the sides of the main façade. In spite of these austere elements, the apse is embellished with slender columns, machicolations, sawtooth motifs, masks and other decorative elements placed around the corbels at the top of the blind arches. Inside, a phytomorphic garland decorates the impost while a triumphal arch rests on pairs of half columns with capitals depicting events and with floral motifs.

The exterior of the chancel followed the late-Romanesque style

The work on the chancel, presbytery, sacristy, cloisters, refectory and canons' chambers spanned the period 1195 to 1215, and progressed more quickly as it was supported by archbishops Ramon de Castellterçol (1194-1198) and Ramon de Rocabertí (1199-1215).

During the tenure of Aspàrec de Barca (1215-1233) the decision was taken to alter the original fabric of the building and adopt a monastic ground plan: a large cloisters —influenced architecturally by the nearby monasteries of Poblet, Santes Creus, Vallbona de les Monges—, five apses (one of them remaining unbuilt due to the location of the cloisters), a spacious transept, slender lantern tower, and three naves covered by ribbed vaults supported by sturdy pillars that all retain their classic proportions.

These alterations were given fresh impetus by Archbishop Pedro de Albalate (1237-1251), who carried out work on the transept, the three initial sections of the central nave and the side naves.

When Bernat d'Olivella (1272-1287) was appointed to the episcopal see, work was carried out on the lantern tower in 1277 and the two final sections of the side naves were completed with their façades be-

←
View of the main apse, transept, bell tower and lantern tower

tween 1266 and 1282, according to the tenets of late-Romanesque architecture. Their unfinished frontispieces were decorated with splayed bullseye windows surmounting the archivolts above the doors. Archbishop Rodrigo Tello (before 1290-1308) was entrusted with the task of enclosing the two final sections of the central nave —which took place some time between 1282 and 1331— and continuing work on the bell tower and main façade. His successors, Guillem de Rocabertí (1309-1315), Jimeno de Luna (1317-1327) and Juan of Aragon (1328-1334), supervised the architectural work and the carving of the central façade, although it was left to Jordi de Déu to complete the sculptural decoration on the exterior, the highest parts of the building and stained-glass windows in 1375.

The cathedral was finally consecrated in 1331 under the archbishop of Tarragona and patriarch of Alexandria, Prince Juan of Aragon. The Black Death brought building work to a halt in 1348 and it didn't resume until the second half of that century. Despite this, the building remained unfinished.

The cathedral is a successful architectural pairing of the early Roman fabric and the new elements added by the new artistic trends of the Gothic era. This combination gives the cathedral a rounded structural harmony and austere intimacy inside, despite the stylistic evolution of the side chapels, the changes in the form of the façade and the fact that the project remained unfinished.

Capitals depicting scenes in the central naves

Above, voussoirs around the apse
Below, discharging pointed arches

Tarragona Cathedral

Main façade

This sumptuous façade, built between 1330 and 1348, has as its centrepiece a magnificent rose window, 11 metres in diameter, with delicate star-shaped tracery. The façade is flanked by two unfinished buttresses and, according to the original plans, was to be crowned by four pinnacles and a gable. They were never added due to the human and economic havoc wrought by the Black Death that devastated Europe in 1348.

It contains elaborate sculptural decorations and has three doors. The majestic Gothic portal in the centre, with its bands of concentric arches and pointed cornice, is unrelated to the original cathedral project. Its design is reminiscent of the portal of Reims Cathedral. It is flanked by two sturdy buttresses crowned by elegant pinnacles. Different-sized slabs of white marble, taken from Roman buildings, are placed around the base. They are decorated with trefoil arches underpinning sculpted figures of characters from the Bible on the jambs and front buttresses.

The Virgin Mary on the mullion

Sculptural ensemble of the Last Judgement

The quality of the sculptures is variable and, according to the original project, there should have been nine more. The mullion in the centre features a marble figure of the Virgin Mary crowned as queen. Slender, smiling, majestic and maternal, she stands at the feet of her reborn son, receiving the faithful as the co-redeemer of humanity. She resembles the figure of the Virgin at Rheims and stands on a footstool depicting scenes from Genesis (the creation of Adam and Eve, the original sin, shame and expulsion from the Garden of Eden). The stylised image of the Virgin and Child leads us to assume that it was carved around 1330 using the shaft of a Roman column.

Above the lintel, flanked by two angel acolytes, and at the base of the tympanum, we see the scene of the Last Judgement —the focal point of the iconographic ensemble of the portal— set out in three sections. The first shows Christ as Supreme Judge and Man of Sorrows, semi-naked without the nimbus containing a cross. He is seated on a throne, barefoot, and shows us

Above the lintel, flanked by two angel acolytes, and at the base of the tympanum, we see the scene of the Last Judgement

the wounds of his crucifixion. He is flanked by the sun and a crescent moon, and two kneeling angels who are carrying the *Arma Christi*: symbols of his Passion and martyrdom. At his feet, a footrest and three angels playing trumpets divide the second scene. Inside its spandrels there are four more —two in flight and two standing— summoning the resurrected emerging from twelve sarcophagi to be judged and carried to the glory of heaven. The third section foretells the moment when the condemned men are led by devils to the gaping jaws of the two-headed monster Leviathan, the enemy of souls and an allegory of hell.

The front of the buttress on the left contains statues of the old man Simeon and the prophets Habakkuk, Jeremiah and Saint John the Baptist. The jambs feature the apostles Matthias, Matthew, John, Philip, James and Paul. The buttress on the right shows the prophets Daniel, Zechariah and Isaiah, followed by Moses and King David. The jambs feature the apostles Judas Thaddeus, Simon, Bartholomew, Thomas, Andrew and Peter.

The sculptural ensemble of the Last Judgement and some of the free-standing images are by Jaume Cascalls, who sculpted the ill-fated royal tombs at Poblet and was one of the most prestigious artists in Catalonia in the second half of the 14th century. He carved the scene around

Detail of one of the leaves of the door with a knocker

1375 helped by his slave Jordi de Déu and the underlings from his workshop. The latter worked on the figures that are of inferior quality.

The leaves of the central door are made of oak covered with iron sheeting secured by bronze nails that alternate with others edged with three tau crosses alluding to Saint Thecla, the patron saint of the Chapter, and three castles referring to the crest of Archbishop Gonzalo Fernández de Heredia (1490-1511) who paid for the work on the door. The embellishments are completed by two simulated wrought-iron hinges and four filigree door knockers on the main doors and the smaller doors set inside them. The ensemble was commissioned by the archbishop and dates from 1510. His crest appears, next to the Cathedral Chapter's, in a repeated motif on the back of the side and central leaves. His tomb stands in front of them.

The two side doors line up with the naves of the Epistle and the Gospel. A Roman sarcophagus, from the Theodosian era and dated 370 to 400 AD, is set into the wall above the right-hand door. The front depicts several events in the life of Christ: the healing of blind Bartimaeus, the suffering of the Canaanite woman, the healing of the crippled man at the pool of Bethesda, the conversion of Zacchaeus, and Christ's triumphal entry into Jerusalem.

Detail of a Roman sarcophagus from the Theodosian era

Biblical characters on the buttresses
on the façade

The tympanum above the porch on the left was completed during the time of Archbishop Olivella (1277). It features the Virgin and Child accompanied by three horses, the Adoration of the Kings, Saint Joseph, the Annunciation, and the announcement to the shepherds. The figures are dynamic and expressive and framed by eight-sided columns, trefoil arches, gables and turrets referring to the heavenly Jerusalem. The leaves of both doors are made of oak covered with copper sheeting and date from the late 19th century. The back is decorated with four shields: the cathedral tau, the shield of the prelate Fernández de Heredia, the keys of Saint Peter referring to the collegiate church of Àger (Lleida), and the shield of its prior, Lorenzo Pérez. There is a rose window above the archivolts of each door. The windows are deeply recessed and feature exquisitely crafted mouldings that frame the modern stained glass.

→
Pinnacles on the façade

Tympanum above the left-hand door

Zoomorphic gargoyles

Images of the prophets

Bell tower

It stands on the outer, north-east-facing corner and is set between the chancel and the eastern wing of the transept. It extends inside over the stretch of vaulting in the side nave where the apsidiole of Saint Olegarius is located. The bell tower is reached via a spiral staircase and consists of three tiers. The first was built in two different phases. The lower section has a square ground plan and was begun in the first half of the 13th century and is, therefore, part of the Romanesque structure. This is borne out by the identical appearance of the ashlars and stonemasons' marks carved into the blocks of stone that can be seen around the base of the bell tower and interior wall of the church. It also houses the austere Romanesque door of Saint Thecla. The first section merges into another that is also square, comprising cushion-shaped ashlars made of grey limestone. They are decorated with the coat of arms of their promoter, the prelate Jimeno de Luna (1316-1327), and the crest of the canon and foreman Hug de Cervelló, a contemporary of his. There is a skylight in each of the walls. The second and third tiers have an octagonal ground plan: the transition from a square to octagon is achieved through four squinches, or conical vaults, reinforced on the outside by buttresses and pinnacles similar to those on the main façade. The second tier houses the clock chamber, which is covered by a ribbed vault, and the third, dating from 1330 and built during the prelateship of Juan of Aragon, houses the bell chamber. The bells can be seen behind the seven mullioned windows carved with masks, friezes with ornate plant motifs, and heraldic emblems referring to Archbishop Juan of Aragon who died in 1334. The ensemble is surmounted by a frontispiece of trifoliate leaves arranged in a zig-zag pattern, gargoyles, pinnacles and a small temple-like structure with four sturdy pillars built in 1511 that houses "La Capona" —the largest of the bells that strikes on the hour and during the call to prayer— and "La dels Quarts", which strikes the quarters of the hour. Both bells were cast in 1509 by Antoni Fenodi.

The bell tower is remarkably high and has several rooms that can house up to nineteen bells. The oldest dates from 1250 and is in the bell chamber, and the most recent hangs in the monks' chamber and was cast by Josep Pomarol in 1867.

← Second and third tier of the bell tower

The bell "Assumpta"

The miniature dome above the lantern tower

The bell "La Capona"

The interior

Once inside the church we can clearly see its basilica-type structure with a Latin-cross ground plan with three naves, an apse, apsidioles, a wide transept and crossing surmounted by a slender, eight-sided lantern tower. The ensemble is covered with ribbed vaults resting on sturdy pillars with a cruciform centre, embellished by twin engaged columns and sculpted capitals decorated with a repertoire of plant and figurative motifs. The right proportion of measurements creates an ensemble of unique beauty that affords views of the spacious transept, as well as the five sections of the central nave, from the entrance and the presbytery. The holy water fonts, once placed at either end of the former retrochoir, are also important due to their structure and the painstaking craftsmanship involved. They date back to the middle of the 13th century and one now stands near the chapel of Saint Thecla and the other by the steps leading into the cloisters. From 1200 onwards, the original interior structure of the cathedral was altered to make way for a series of chapels inside the apses or between the buttresses. They encroached on spaces in the retrochoir and resulted in the dismantling of the fabric of the walls. The different patrons and donors built and made endowments for their chapels so they could be used as family tombs. Depending on the time they were built, they were in harmony with the characteristic style of the church or created different styles that would enrich the interior of the building architecturally.

Holy water fonts

Side nave of the Gospel

Corinthian capitals in the nave of the Gospel

Capitals depicting scenes and cymatia in the crossing

Holy water font

Main door seen from the inside

- Chancel and presbytery
  - A High altarpiece
  - B Tomb of Archbishop Juan of Aragon
  - C Apse chapel of Saint Mary or Tailors' chapel
  - D Apse chapel of Saint Olegarius
- Main sacristy
- Treasury
- Transept
  - E Chapels in the left arm of the transept
  - F Chapels in the right arm of the transept
- Central and side naves
  - G Early choir
  - H Grand organ
  - I Chapels in the left-hand side naves
  - J Chapels in the left retrochoir
  - K Chapels in the right-hand side nave
  - L Chapels in the right retrochoir
- Cloisters
  - M Chapels in the cloisters
- Present-day chapter house
- The canons' old refectory

Chancel and presbytery

The late 12th-century apse in the cathedral chancel has a pointed quarter-sphere vault, or cul-de-four, a pointed triumphal arch and two rows of rounded side arches. Some of the capitals feature detailed depictions of scenes from the Bible and allegorical and fantastic motifs; others are embellished with plant motifs that evoke Roman designs. The structure and decoration of the cornices follow the Romanesque tradition, which can also be seen in the central apse, apsidioles and splayed windows. The bases of the columns are in the Attic style and decorated with flat mouldings. Building work on this part of the church had reached the top of the capitals, but towards 1195 the builders decided on an important change of plan: they placed a pilaster above the capitals that made it possible to cover the space with a higher vault with pointed arches, in order to adapt the proportions of the church to the new tenets of French Gothic cathedrals. The new building measures and techniques were then applied to the transept, central nave and side naves. The prelates Berenguer de Vilademuls (1174-1194) and Ramón de Rocabertí (1199-1215) were actively involved in extending the church. With the aid of generous contributions from the monarchs, they managed different systems of financial resources to proceed with building work.

A section of the Gothic choir stalls can be seen in the presbytery

Other highlights include the splendid 13th-century Romanesque floor in the central apse and part of the presbytery, made using the Roman *opus sectile* technique that creates geometric compositions using pieces of limestone and coloured marble, and two Roman inscriptions —L. CAECINAE on the right-hand wall next to the niche containing the relics, and another on the left, hidden behind the carillon— as well as several tombstones dating from the 14th to 19th centuries commemorating the archbishops of this metropolitan see.

A section of the Gothic choir stalls that occupied part of the central nave until 1963 are another important feature of the presbytery. During the restoration process in 2012, frescoes representing textile hangings were revealed. The side walls, near the high altarpiece, are decorated with stencilled floral motifs arranged in horizontal rows and resembling fabric. The design of this fabric can be seen in the clothing worn by people depicted in several altarpieces made during the 14th and 15th centuries.

←
Presbytery and chancel

Flamboyant-Gothic door at the side of the presbytery

Above, mural replicating floral fabric
Below, detail of the Romanesque floor

Interior of the main apse

Baroque tabernacle behind the high altarpiece

High altarpiece

In 1388, during the prelateship of Ènnec de Vallterra (1380-1407), general provisions were made for the building of a high altarpiece worthy of Tarragona Cathedral. From this year onwards, bequests, collections and the personal contributions of prelates, canons, diners and beneficiaries were put together so work could be carried out. On 8th March 1426, an official agreement was signed between Archbishop Dalmau de Mur i de Cervelló (1419-1431), the Cathedral Chapter and master sculptor Pere Joan who, a year later, began working on the project in his workshop. On 5th April 1429, the archbishop laid the foundation stone.

The altarpiece is made of alabastrine and was completed in 1434. It is a magnificent example of Catalan gothic sculpture. It stands on a sturdy limestone plinth decorated with curling thistle leaves and figures of children, dogs, and the crests of Archbishop Pere de Sagarriga (right) and, its promoter, Archbishop Dalmau de Mur (left), and the emblem of the Chapter (centre) with angels beneath. Above it, the superb high-relief predella depicts six scenes from the life and martyrdom of Saint Thecla, sculpted with great subtlety and virtuosity, against a cobalt blue background.

Detail of the plinth

Central section of the predella

The dead Christ

Nicodemus

The first scene shows Saint Paul preaching. He is sitting in his chair under a canopy held by angels. Next to him, Saint Thecla listens to him in wrapt attention while Thamyris pulls her away from the group. This scene is followed by the martyrdom of Saint Thecla at the stake. She is semi-naked, smiling and held up by two boy angels while the flames swirl around the heads of the six executioners. In the next scene, twelve elegant spectators on a grandstand watch two lionesses fighting. With a demure expression, they look at the saint praying and the wild beasts that have been miraculously tamed. The martyrdom scene is divided by the tabernacle chancel where an angel appears holding up the Holy Shroud with the dying Christ worshipped by the Virgin Mary, Saint John the Baptist, Nicodemus and Joseph of Arimathea separated by angels. The story continues, according to the *Apocryphal Acts of Paul and Thecla*, showing the martyr under water, with sea lions, or in a pond. Thecla is depicted blessing the water with poisonous reptiles slithering away from her. The predella features two episodes not depicted on the front of the Romanesque high altar. One depicts the torment of the saint on the outskirts of the city of Antioch. She is tied to a pair of oxen being whipped by her torturers so they will tear her apart. Miraculously immobilised she sits on the ground in an attitude of prayer looking heavenwards and is freed when the ropes break. She is surrounded by soldiers, magistrates tearing their robes, judges and spectators. The next episode refers to the miraculous discovery of Saint Thecla's arm as described in the *Tarragona Breviary*. It was found among the crags that concealed her tomb, and picked up by the prelate in the presence of the clergy and faithful. The relic offered by King Ixion of Armenia Minor to the Church of Tarragona, through the mediation of King Jaime II in 1321, is thought to be part of this arm. The scenes alternate with eight images of virgins and the objects used in their martyrdom. These enable us to identify Saint Catherine, Saint Barbara, Saint Lucy, Saint Eulalia of Barcelona, Saint Agatha, Saint Anastasia (?), Saint Cecilia and Saint Agnes. The sculptor Pere Joan revealed the full extent of his exquisite skill on this predella with its harmonious compositions, detailed clothing, variety of hair styles and gallery of expressive portraits which retain traces of their original gilding and discreet colour palette.

The sculptor Pere Joan revealed the full extent of his exquisite skill in this predella

1

4

1 Saint Paul preaching

2 Torment by fire

3 Tamed lions

4 The reptiles slither away from Saint Thecla

5 The saint, dragged along by an ox

6 The discovery of her arm

2

3

5

6

The centre of the altarpiece houses the image of the Virgin and Child, carved out of two blocks of polychrome alabaster divided at the waist. She is holding a silver lily in her hand donated by a worshipper in 1582 and flanked by carvings of Saint Thecla and Saint Paul beneath filigree canopies, pinnacles, openwork crests, spires and backrests painted with blue pigment and gilded by Valentí Montoliu in 1447. Around them, twelve reliefs below smaller canopies reproduce scenes from the childhood of Christ (Annunciation, birth, Epiphany, presentation in the temple), his Passion (Last Supper, flogging, Way to Calvary, crucifixion), Resurrection and Ascension, to which we add the episode from Pentecost and the Coronation of the Virgin.

The centre of the altarpiece houses the image of the Virgin and Child, carved out of two blocks of polychrome alabaster

There are two doors on either side of the altarpiece. They are part of its structure, rendered in the same style and have elegant Flamboyant-Gothic lattice windows capped by elaborate corbels where we find the images of the archbishops of Tarragona, Saint Olegarius and Saint Fructuosus. They are placed in front of twin windows with a brocade-like decoration made to resemble stained-glass windows. On the frontispieces stand the images of Saint Michael the Archangel and the Guardian Angel carved by Perris Austris and added in 1557. They were gilded and coloured by the Italian painter Pietro Paolo de Montalbergo. In the apse, behind the altarpiece, we can admire a smiling Saint Michael —framed by the intrados of the lobulate portal with its leaf decorations— protecting the small shrine, or aedicule, housing the baroque tabernacle and the Holy Sacrament. It is made of marble and flanked by two niches housing the Sacred Forms, the Holy Oils, the *Lignum Crucis* and the *Santa Fimbria*. It was sculpted by Isidre Espinalt Serrarica between 1696 and 1697 at the behest of Archbishop Josep Llinàs (1695-1710).

Saint Paul next to Christ on Calvary

The Adoration of the Kings

The Last Supper

High altar

The high altar was made under the patronage of Archbishop Aspàreg de la Barca (1215-1233). It is highly likely that it originally stood in the centre of the semi-circle of the apse, edged by stone benches resembling choir stalls. This appears to be borne out by the square flagstones that intercut the original flooring of the presbytery. The altar was subsequently moved to its current location when the Gothic altarpiece was put in place. To ensure it was in proportion with the new altarpiece, the altar table, or *mensa*, was extended at the sides, and columns were added to hold it up. The altar rests on two wide steps edged by an ornate, archaic-looking element that may come from another pre-existing monument. It is made of white marble and has a splendid frontal, resembling ivory, sculpted around 1220. It is considered one of the finest examples of Catalan Romanesque sculpture. The central mandorla depicts the

It is considered one of the finest examples of Catalan Romanesque sculpture

High altar

Holy Trinity: Christ blessing Saint Thecla, God the Father symbolised by the *Dextera Dei* set inside a nimbus and the Holy Spirit in the form of a dove beating its wings. The casings of the side panels depict eight scenes from Saint Thecla's martyrdom, as described in the *Apocryphal Acts of Paul and Thecla*. On the left, beneath a clypeus with leaf motifs and a square frame housing two lions facing each other, we see Theocleia leading Thecla's betrothed Thamyris by the hand, pointing to her daughter who is listening at her window to Paul preaching in the house of Onesiphorus about the vow of chastity taken by Thecla despite her betrothal. Afterwards, Thecla is accused by the governor's court and condemned to be burned at the stake. Nevertheless, she makes a miraculous escape. On the right we see the Saint praying among tamed wild beasts and protected by the *Dextera Dei* and an angel. Following this, a group of women lead her to the mansion of Queen Tryphaena to seek her protection. After this, the saint appears flung into the waters of the amphitheatre filled with vermin and poisonous snakes. The final episode depicts the death of Thecla in Seleucia, surrounded by her next of kin while two angels deliver her soul to heaven in the guise of a dove.

Detail of the mandorla: Christ blessing Saint Thecla

Tomb of Juan of Aragon

A very wide barrel vault houses the parallepiped-shaped sarcophagus supported by two leonine figures. On the top lies a sculpture of Juan of Aragon, archbishop of Tarragona, patriarch of Alexandria and son of King Jaime II and Blanche of Naples. This arcosolium consists of a segmental arch decorated with mouldings, instead of the pointed arch characteristic of the time, capitals with flowers, stone openwork around the intrados and leaf carvings on the extrados, faces with floral crowns, symbols of the hope of resurrection, and two slender pinnacles at the sides.

Archbishop Juan of Aragon

The recumbent effigy of the prelate, who died at the early age of 33, is dressed in pontiff's robes. It is considered a masterpiece of Spanish Gothic sculpture and is attributed to a follower of the Italian sculptor Tino di Camaino. The effigy was sculpted around 1337 with a deftness of touch seen in the stylised face that exudes a beatific serenity and peace. The natural and harmonious plasticity of the liturgical vestments revealed in the chasuble, mitre and gloves, together with the painstakingly rendered sculptural and ornamental details on the top of the crosier, reveal the mastery of their creator. The frontal of the sarcophagus is decorated with a carved voussoir, leaves and a plethora of laudatory Gothic inscriptions alluding to the ascetic and charitable life of the prelate, and his gifts as a preacher.

Around the tomb you'll find statues of Saint Thecla; Saint Elizabeth of Hungary, Juan of Aragon's father's sister; Saint Louis, king of France, his uncle on his mother's side; Saint Louis, bishop of Toulouse, the brother of his mother Blanche of Naples and son of Charles of Sicily; and Saint Fructuosus. The high relief on the front of the wall depicts the entry into glory of the soul of the deceased being received by Christ and gathered up in a shroud by two boy angels. Together with the mausoleums in the chapel of the Immaculate Conception, this is one of the most outstanding in the cathedral due to the materials used, technical skill and iconographic repertoire.

The ensemble was carved in white marble and is located on the side wall on the right-hand side of the presbytery beneath the mullioned Gothic niche, surmounted by a pediment with leaf decorations, where the reliquary of Saint Thecla was kept until Napoleon's troops laid siege to the cathedral. It was built around 1328 at the behest of Juan of Aragon who had received the relic through the good offices of his father in 1321. He stipulated that, after his death, which occurred on 19th August 1334, his tomb be placed beneath the protomartyr's relics. It is crowned by a sculpture probably depicting Saint Elizabeth of Hungary accompanied by Saint Paul and Saint Thecla.

← Arcosolium with the tomb

Apse chapel of Saint Mary, or Tailors' chapel

This chapel is dedicated to the worship of the Virgin Mary and its iconographic repertoire is part of the devotional phenomenon created by the Cistercians and adopted by mendicant orders during the 13th century. This is the most sumptuous chapel in the cathedral due to its rich architectural, sculptural and pictorial decorations. It stands on the site of the demolished Romanesque apsidiole that once occupied the left-hand side nave. The curve of its outline can still be seen on the floor. The conversion of the semicircular apse into a polygonal, fully Gothic one began towards the middle of the 14th century at the behest of the Brotherhood of Presbyters. There is no record that the English master builder Reinhard de Fonoll was involved at the start of the work. In 1359, the final payments were made for the stained-glass windows. The archbishop at the time was Pere de Clasquerí (1358-1380), who had brought the project to fruition together with the canons Guillem d'Anglesola, Saportella and Bernat d'Albió, who also supervised building work. Their crests decorate the walls. It is likely that Fonoll became involved in the chapel project as *magister operis* around 1361 following the bitter confrontations between the developers' families that were resolved by the prelate Clasquerí. The Flamboyant-Gothic design of the architectural elements on the false windows, the gallery of the *pueri cantores*, the sacristy, and the door connecting the central apse and high altar are all attributed to the architect. The chapel has a hexagonal ground plan and a star-shaped ribbed vault. At the base of the arches there are pairs of sculptures under small canopies and images on the corners. A third of the way up is a frieze of blind ogee arches underpinned by corbels bearing effigies. Above it is a protruding ledge with subtle floral motifs, and a balcony with stylised tracery on its arches reminiscent of the galleries in the English cathedrals of Winchester, Wells and Exeter where the choirboys would sing. The leaded windows, by Guillem de Latungart, who hailed from Coutances (Normandy), were fitted in 1359. The emblem of the Cathedral Chapter, one of the two annunciations and two angels framed by trefoils are the only original sections to survive.

In 1388 this chapel was transferred to the Tailors' Guild by the Brotherhood of Presbyters so they could see to its upkeep

The altarpiece is made of polychrome limestone worked in high relief circa 1365/67 at the workshop of a sculptor associated with the Norman artist Aloi de Montbrai. It depicts three thematic cycles framed by architectural elements: the childhood of Christ, stories of the Passion,

→ Chapel altarpiece

and stories of the Virgin Mary culminating in her glorification. The Virgin with her son in her arms is depicted free standing and presides over the series of reliefs carved by one of Montbrai's associates and supervised by him. The series of scenes is set against a frieze resembling a small-scale predella with ten figures of martyrs fixed to the wall, two unidentified crests, and two Atlases on the sides. Among the plethora of sculptures decorating the gallery, Montbrai may have carved the group with the Virgin and archangel Gabriel, Saint Margaret of Antioch and Catherine of Alexandria, the arches and reliefs around them, and the corbels inside the sacristy. The white marble *mensa* of the altar rests on a central drum. They both come from Roman remains found close to the cathedral. The *mensa* is supported by four Romanesque columns. The altar was consecrated on 31st December 1367.

←
Altar, altarpiece and choir gallery

The frescos replicating stained-glass windows on the left-hand wall, depicting Saint Judas Thaddeus, Saint James the Less and his mother Mary, are attributed to the Master of Santa Coloma de Queralt (Tarragona), or Pere de Tarragona. They were discovered in 1983 and date from the second half of the 14th century.

The right-hand side wall houses the polychrome wooden burial casket of Archbishop Pere de Clasquerí, which can be dated to 1388, flanked by images of Saint Paul and Saint Thecla. The extraordinary paintings over the lintel of the door leading into the presbytery show the prelate dressed in pontiff's attire kneeling before the Virgin and Baby Jesus. They are attributed to the mural painter, Guillem de Timor.

A gallery was added in 1499, above the door leading into the cloisters, to house the organ that accompanied the services held at the altar of the Virgin. In 1388, this chapel was transferred to the Tailors' Guild by the Brotherhood of Presbyters so they could see to its upkeep. This accounts for its nickname ('sastre' is Catalan for tailor).

Relief on the altarpiece: Pentecost

Mural paintings and burial casket of Archbishop Pere de Clasquerí

Apse chapel of Saint Olegarius

Apse chapel of Saint Olegarius

This chapel occupies the Romanesque apsidiole built around 1200, probably during the tenure of Archbishop Ramon de Rocabertí (1199-1215). It stands in the right-hand side nave and is spanned by vaulting with important capitals dating from the 12th century. The bell tower stands directly above it. The chapel originally housed an altar dedicated to Saint John the Baptist and Saint John the Evangelist. In 1375 the Tarragona-born sculptor Dalmau Balcells carved a stone altarpiece at the behest of the saddler Berenguer d'Albió, which was replaced by another dedicated to Saint Thecla painted in 1527 to honour the patron saint of Tarragona and Saint Maginus. These altarpieces and carvings survived until 1775, the year the new chapel dedicated to the protomartyr was built in the nave of the Epistle, an event that led to the altarpiece being dismantled and replaced by a new one dedicated to Saint Olegarius. It was carved by Francesc Bonifàç Massó in 1776 together with the sculptures of Saint Eulalia of Barcelona, Saint Aloysius Gonzaga, two narrative panels and some heads of angels that survive today. The sculptural ensemble was dismantled in 1936 and almost entirely destroyed in 1937. The current altar dates from the early 20th century. Originally housed in the chapel of the Holy Christ of Health, it was moved to its current location in 2012. A statue of Saint Olegarius stands on the altar.

Corbel with effigy

On the vaulting we can see the primitive ribbon motifs, and on the column on the left-hand side traces of colour of the frescoes resembling drapes that decorated the lower part of the apse. Next to them is one of the walls that flanked the door leading into the former choir stalls built during the time of Archbishop Jimeno de Luna (1316-1327) and the canon and foreman Hug de Cervelló. It is surmounted by a frieze of blind arches, corbels with effigies and heraldic emblems.

Main sacristy

←
Detail of the tapestry from the *Story of Joseph* series

Built between the end of the 12th and early 13th centuries, the sacristy has a rectangular ground plan and pointed barrel vault hidden by the framework of a flat wooden ceiling dating from the 18th century over which are placed cupboards containing ancient liturgical vestments. The space it currently occupies, and the adjacent chamber, were converted into a chapel in the 14th century. This is borne out by the coffered ceiling in the treasury, which was part of the rood screen, now vanished, and the credence in the wall next to the door leading into the central apse. Two windows were opened in the wall when it was decided to use the space as a sacristy. One dates from 1597 and the other from the late 19th century. There is another window in the adjacent room and all three open onto the cloisters above their corresponding centre line.

Beneath the canopy in the chancel we find the notable baroque carving of Christ dying on the cross with its pronounced *contrapposto*. The carving dates from the 18th century and comes from the church of Sant Miquel del Pla in Tarragona. It was placed in the sacristy in 1931. A tapestry in two sections hangs on the east wall depicting the episode from the *Story of Joseph* when he was sold by his brothers to the Ishmaelites in Dothan in exchange for twenty pieces of silver, and his subsequent exaltation by the Pharaoh. It was made in Brussels at the beginning of the 16th century, donated to the archbishop Alfonso of Aragon (1513-1514) and is part of the Cathedral Chapter collection.

↓
On the left, Christ on the cross

On the right, water basin

Treasury

←
Coffering

The treasury, which opened in 1930, is reached from the main sacristy through a Gothic doorway with an ogee lintel placed in front of the segmental arch that once underpinned the now-vanished rood screen and was an integral part of the sacristy. Once inside, we see the magnificent mid-14th-century Moorish-style, Gothic coffered ceiling in polychrome wood. It fits in perfectly with the structural patterns of Catalan ceilings providing a faster, more affordable alternative to stone. Its frame, consisting of beams, cross beams, joists and fifty-four square panels, is underpinned by anthropomorphic corbels depicting grotesque figures. The ceiling was probably completed around 1360. The iconographic programme repeats the emblem of the Saportella dynasty with the crest of the Chapter alternating with rosettes and discs with a spiral motif redolent of the Mozarabic style, fauna, flora and scenes featuring human beings. The ensemble, picked out in bright colours, draws inspiration from Gothic and Moorish repertoires and Renaissance grotesques.

The glass-fronted latticework cabinets are used to store a number of liturgical objects, especially silverware. Particularly noteworthy are the collection of chalices, reliquaries, processional maces and bishops' crosiers from the 18th to 20th centuries; the casket for the Monument to Maundy Thursday carved by the Tarragona-born silversmith Gaspar Arandes Alomar in 1685; the processional biers and the monumental neo-Gothic monstrance, made in Barcelona in the 19th century.

The most outstanding pieces from the cathedral treasury disappeared during the Napoleonic invasion in 1811.

Casket for the Monument to Maundy Thursday

Transept

This is the transverse part of a cathedral that crosses the main nave at a right angle and gives visitors a wonderful spatial perspective. The transept was completed around 1259 and is 52.5 metres long by 15 metres wide. The space between the transept and the nave is known as a crossing, and is the result of the fresh momentum given to building the cathedral when the initial project was changed. The side façade of the church defined the boundary of the southern arm of the crossing, which was shorter than the northern arm where the wall that formed the base of the canons' refectory —one of the oldest medieval buildings in the ensemble— stood. The lantern tower stands above the crossing and is the most attractive, aesthetically pleasing and symbolic part as it traditionally evokes the divine space inhabited by God. It stands 32 metres high at its keystone, has an octagonal ground plan and is covered with a groin vault. It is inset with stained-glass windows and underpinned by squinches that decrease in size. Its style is early Gothic, or characteristic of the transition from the Romanesque to the ogival arch, the change from the original structure being seen in the truncated cornice that was part of the initial project and decorates the right-hand front wall of the transept.

Crossing with the lantern tower

There are two rose window on the north-west wall and south-east wall of the transept. They have star-shaped tracery and leaded stained glass dating from the late 14th and early 15th centuries. In the south-east window, the light shining through the central oculus allows us to see the image of the Virgin and Child and four angels playing musical instruments. The sixteen radiating panels feature the Tree of Jesse and heads wearing crowns in reference to the kings of Judah, as well as eight maidens offering the crowns to the Virgin as the Queen of Heaven and Earth. The north-western rose window depicts the Resurrection of Christ with the soldiers at the foot of his tomb. The sixteen radiating panels feature the heads of the apostles alluding to preaching the Kingdom of God, which alternate with other figurative, ornamental motifs. The funeral caskets supported by corbels on the side walls of the chapel of the Holiest were placed there in the 14th century. They contain the mortal remains of the archbishops who had been buried nearby before the current cathedral was built.

North-western rose window
with the Resurrection of Christ

→
View of the chapel of Saint Barbara
and the Tailors' chapel

Chapels in the left arm of the transept

Chapel of Saint Barbara

Formerly dedicated to Saint Augustine, this Gothic chapel originally had a stone altar and altarpiece dated around 1362. It stood inside what was originally taken up by a smaller fifth apse. Only the image of Saint Barbara survives and is now part of the Diocesan Museum's collections. The chapel was refurbished by the archdeacon of Vila-seca (Tarragona), Bernat Rufaca i Anglesola, to be used as his tomb. His crest decorates the keystone and walls. The frontispiece has a portal of blind trefoil arches and an artistic gable, a triumphal arch with tracery on the intrados and plant motifs on the reredos. The chapel has a polygonal ground plan , a groin vault and a keystone in a poor state of repair. It houses the baroque wooden altarpiece gilded with a profusion of leaves, floral motifs and corbels at the sides. It is dated 1765. The canon and hospitaller Francesc-Xavier Foguet Aldomar paid for the baroque ornamental ensemble to frame an oil painting of the saint flanked by two sculptures representing Saint Anthony of Padua and Saint Blaise. They are by an unknown artist, as are the oil paintings of Saint Barbara of Bithynia, the Franciscan saint at the top of the altarpiece, Saint Francis Xavier dying on the Chinese island of Shangchuan, placed on the predella, and the tower on the front of the altar, the symbol of Saint Barbara. The gilding of the splendid altarpiece framing these oils was also paid for by the archdeacon. The grille was fitted in 1980.

→ Altarpiece of Saint Barbara

Detail of the front of the altarpiece

Chapel of Saints Cosmas and Damian

The worship of the Physician Saints at the cathedral dates back to the second half of the 15th century. This chapel could not have been any deeper due to the thickness of the wall and was initially dedicated to Saint Blaise and Saint Susanna as a result of the prebends allotted by Bernat Solsona and Bernat Desgrau in 1362 and 1389, respectively. The existence of an altar in honour of Saints Cosmas and Damian can be deduced from a bequest in a will dated 1466 in favour of building this chapel under the custodianship of the Guild of Physicians, Pharmacists and Barbers. It was built in 1591 on a small rectangular ground plan in the Renaissance style to a project by the architect Pere Blai. Particularly noteworthy are the imposing limestone doorway with its rounded arch, the compound pilasters and the frontispiece divided in two by two voluminous volutes. The panelled vault decorated with acanthus leaves is supported by the cornice around the perimeter and overhangs the gilded wooden altarpiece with its Solomonic columns, leaves, cherubims and two niches housing the carvings of the saints who are the dedicatees of the chapel: Cosmas is looking at a flask containing the patient's urine while holding the *vademecum* with his formulas and notes; Damian is carrying a box containing medicines and surgical material. A smaller altarpiece above it frames an oil painting with the image of Bishop Saint Liborius, the protector of kidney diseases. It is crowned by a sterilising pan for nursing instruments. The frontal of the altar is polychrome with two kraters filled with flowers. The year 1712 can be read on both sides of the altar table. The wrought iron railing was fitted in 1880.

Detail of the front of the altarpiece

Chapel of the Holy Sacrament

During the prelature of the illustrious humanist and lawyer Antonio Agustín Albanell (1576-1586), the southern part of the canons' refectory —built with a pointed barrel vault in the late 12th and early 13th centuries— was remodelled and converted into a chapel between 1582 and 1592. The refurbishment was carried out by Bernat Cassany, the cathedral's master builder, in association with the priest Jaume Amigó. Cassany died shortly after work had commenced and he was replaced by the architect Pere Blai who completed the project. This beautiful example of Renaissance architecture is reached through an understated classicist portal flanked by two grey granite Roman columns taken from the ruined church of Sant Pere Sescelades. The chapel has a rectangular ground plan and a semi-spherical dome resting on a drum decorated with images of the saints associated with the Holy Sacrament, busts alluding to the virgin martyrs in the chapel of Saint Ursula, or Baptistry chapel, where the Holy Sacrament was once kept, along with several figures from the Old Testament. The features of the latter group of figures suggest they were manufactured in the 18th century.

The iconographic repertoire in the chancel features scenes from the Old and New Testaments alluding to Passover and Easter set into surrounds made of jasper from Tortosa. On the left we see, from top to bottom, the exterminating angel kept at bay by the blood of the lamb of God, the immolation of the Paschal lamb, and Christ consecrating the wine at the Last Supper. On the right is a scene depicting the manna sent by God to the Israelites during their crossing of the desert, the procession of the Ark of the Alliance and the breaking of the bread when Christ met the disciples on the road to Emmaus.

Paintings in the chancel

High reliefs on the doors of the tabernacle

The panels were painted on slate by the Dutch artist Isaac Hermes Vermey around 1587 and were a truly unique artwork in 16th-century Catalonia. The high reliefs on the doors of the tabernacle show scenes from the Passion of Christ. They were designed by Gaspar de Lira, a silversmith from Medina del Campo (Valladolid), and cast and carved by Felip Voltes, from La Selva del Camp (Tarragona), in 1588. The sculptures flanking the tabernacle are by Domenico Albrioni and Nicolás Larraut and date from 1587.

Above the altar inside the Romanesque wall on the left-hand side is an oil painting depicting the Coronation of the Virgin. It was purchased by the principal archbishop from the Genovese artist Luca Cambiaso who painted it between 1583 and 1585. The founder's tomb

Altarpiece of Saint Martin

was designed by Pere Blai and carved in 1592 by Isaac Alfard Vermey in alabastrine marble from Sarral (Tarragona) based on designs by Andrea del Verrocchio. The altarpiece above the altar by the entrance dates from 1622 and features a carving of Saint Martin of Tours and scenes from the life of the saint attributed to the Aragonese painter Tomás de Argüello.

The altars on the right-hand wall contains a 17th-century painting showing Saint Charles Borromeo praying to the angel who is pointing to a nail from Christ's crucifixion. It was donated by Miquel-Joan Fivaller, archdeacon of Vila-seca. Next to it is a polychrome altarpiece dedicated to Saint Augustine by Francesc Bonifàç Massó put in place in 1795 and paid for by Canon Jaume Ferrer de Santjoan.

Chapels in the right arm of the transept

Chapel of Saint Luke

The chapel of Saint Luke the Evangelist, formerly dedicated to Saint Peter and the place where the Monument to Maundy Thursday once stood, is situated in the Romanesque side apsidiole built around 1200. The original altar table survives, supported by four Romanesque columns in a poor state of repair that attest to its age. In the late 14th century, a brotherhood named after Saint Luke was founded under the patronage of the city's procurators and notaries. It houses a baroque altarpiece with twin Solomonic columns on either side, their shafts decorated with cherubims and birds pecking at bunches of grapes. The altarpiece dates from 1679 and frames an oil painting with an image of the saint in ecstasy at the sight of the Virgin Mary cradling the Christ Child in her arms. The painting is attributed to the painter from Cornudella (Tarragona), Josep Juncosa. The panels on the podiums of the columns feature Saint Augustine and Saint Ambrose. The predella shows Saint Paul at the Areopagus in Athens and iconoclastic scenes. The top section features the apostles Peter and Paul surmounted by a finial with the heart of Jesus crowned with thorns. The latter is one of the oldest known icons of this devotion, which was widely disseminated following the manifestation of Christ to Saint Margaret Mary Alacoque in 1673.

→ Altarpiece of Saint Luke

Eastern arm of the transept

Chapels built by Canon Antoni Barceló

Three chapels were attached to the wall at the right-hand end of the transept, below the 14th-century rose window. They are attributed to the Girona-born architect Pere Compte and were built between 1494 and 1500 under the patronage of the canon Antoni Barceló whose crest, together with the Chapter's, is repeated on the frontispiece. The chapels were built in the Flamboyant-Gothic style with similarities in type and ornamentation to buildings designed by Compte in Valencia. The chapels consist of a single section, resembling a clerestory, with tracery, flower motifs and leaves carved out of the arches, and twisted columns and narrative corbels surmounted by a stepped frontispiece. The three chapels were badly damaged when they were plundered by the Napoleonic troops commanded by General Suchet during the siege of Tarragona between 1808 and 1813.

Chapel of Our Lady of the Rosary

The chapel on the left-hand side was originally dedicated to Saint Stephen, a title dating back to 1275 when the canon-hospitaller Guillem Esteve set up a stipend under the advocacy of the protomartyr. In 1865 the chapel was assigned to the Brotherhood of Our Lady of the Rosary, who, in 1891, installed a neo-Gothic gilded wooden altarpiece designed by the diocesan architect Ramon Salas Ricomà, which was destroyed in 1937. The current statues of the Virgin Mary with her son date from 1950 and were made by two Tarragona-based artists: the sculptor Lluís Maria Saumells Panadés, who hailed from Gironella near Barcelona, and the Girona-born painter Sadurní García Anguera who carried out the polychrome work. The vaulting is blue with gilded stars on the severies and simulated marble ribs. The central keystone features a relief of Saint Stephen, its original dedicatee, who shows us the stones used to kill him. The grille was fitted in 1919.

Chapel of the Holy Christ of Health

This is the only chapel in the cathedral dedicated to the same saint as when it was built and where people worship the Gothic effigy of the Holy Christ of Health. It is Flemish in influence and was carved in the early 16th

Chapel of Our Lady of the Rosary

century and paid for by Canon Barceló. Our Lady of Sorrows and Saint John the Evangelist are Gothic carvings dating from the second half of the 15th century and were originally placed inside a neoclassical altarpiece made by Vicenç Roig Besora in 1801. The vaulting is polychrome in a similar style to the three chapels above and the central keystone reproduces the *Maiestas Domini*.

Chapel of Saint Thomas Aquinas

This chapel was formerly dedicated to Saint Bartholomew who was worshipped in the central panels of an altarpiece that is now missing. In 1853 an altar was built dedicated to Saint Philomena in front of the pre-existing neoclassical canopy. It was made by Vicenç Roig Besora under the patronage of Chapter member, Josep de Vilallonga. From 1933 onwards, the chapel housed the image of Saint Thomas. The ensemble was destroyed in 1937, with the exception of the image of the saint carved in 1832 by the aforementioned sculptor. Since 1944, the chapel has housed a gilded wooden neo-Gothic altarpiece built in 1877 and paid for by Canon Joan Baptista Pedrals Arqués where the image of the Dominican saint is worshipped. The altarpiece was occasionally placed above the cathedral's high altar to display the blessed sacrament inside the monumental monstrance paid for by Archbishop Tomàs Costa Fornaguera (1889-1911).

Chapel of the Holy Christ of Health

Chapel of Saint Thomas Aquinas

Central and side naves

There is a sweeping panoramic view of the cathedral interior from behind the main portal and the steps leading up to the high altar. The central nave is 104 metres long, 16 metres wide and 26 metres high. The keystone of the lantern tower stands 32 metres above the ground. The side naves are 7.5 metres wide and 13 metres high. The central nave and side naves are divided into sections and have ribbed vaults with mouldings that converge on sculpted capitals. They are supported by cruciform columns with engaged columns around them with narrative, zoomorphic and phytomorphic capitals. Two keystones in the central nave and a couple of mouldings in the side naves are polychrome, just like the spandrel of the severies and the base of the transverse arch. The windows in the chancel are Romanesque and the others are Gothic. From the 14th to 18th centuries, a number of chapels were built inside the side naves in different styles.

Side nave
of the Epistle

Early choir

← Chair with a triple canopy

The cathedral choir was originally placed around the semi-circular apse and behind the altar. It was made of stone in the manner of a long stone pew. Once the vaulting had been completed, the choir was moved to the central nave during the prelateship of Rodrigo Tello (1288-1308), where it occupied the first three sections of the transept. The side walls were built between 1317 and 1327. The magnificent stalls made from Flanders oak were sculpted by the Zaragoza-born sculptor Francisco Gomar between 1479 and 1493 when Pedro de Urrea (1445-1489) was archbishop. The canopies and backrests are decorated with lavish Gothic tracery and marquetry that repeat, like a frieze, the archbishop's emblem above the seats. The scrolls on the armrests are decorated with floral, mythological and zoomorphic motifs. A pontifical seat is at the head of the presbytery stalls, and another, with a triple canopy, is the centrepiece of the stalls in the central nave. They were carved in the Plateresque style by Juan de Tours and Enrique de Borgoña in 1534 and were paid for by Lorenzo Pérez, bishop of Neapolis and auxiliary bishop of Tarragona (1502-1542). The walls at the sides of the door leading into the choir —surmounted by the sculptural grouping of the Annunciation made between 1292 and 1323— were dismantled in 1962, to free up space in the central nave. In 1963, the iconographic repertoire with interesting corbels that decorated the walls and lower stalls was transferred to the intercolumns at the sides in the first section of the current presbytery. The mural and sculptural ensemble in the retrochoir was built in the early 1300s, during the tenure of Archbishop Jimeno de Luna (1316-1327).

Details of the choir stalls

Central nave: choir stalls and grand organ

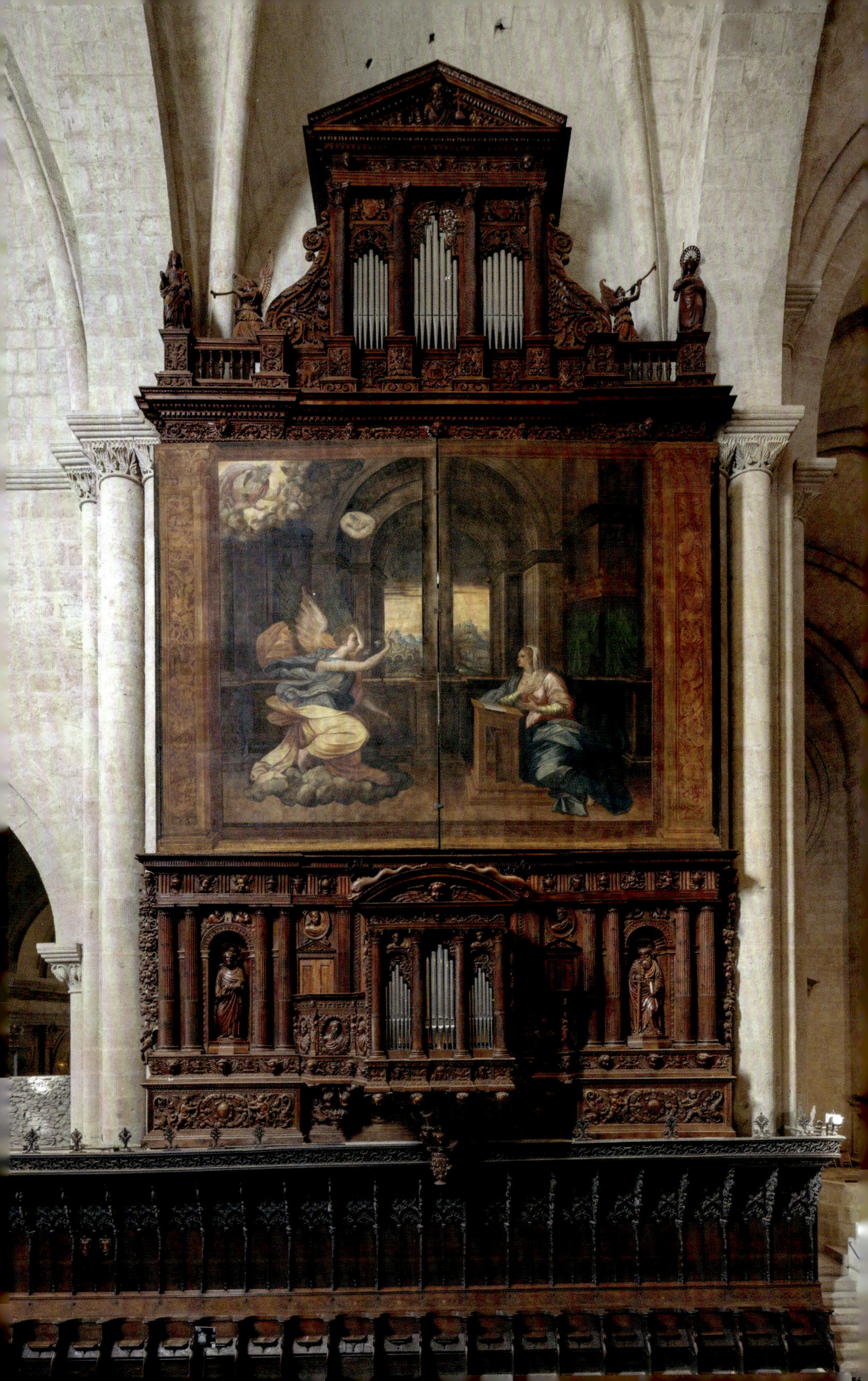

Grand organ

We know from the first records, dated 1164, that several organs were placed in different areas of the cathedral and used to accompany the different religious ceremonies. The current organ is monumental in scale and was conceived as a spectacular altarpiece. Built in the 16th century, it occupies the left-hand wall of the central nave above a section of the choir stalls. The organ is 20 metres high and 9 metres wide and is considered truly unique among the existing cathedral organs in Spain due to its scale, style, decorative motifs and quality of its sculptures. The casing, which contains the metal organ pipes and is covered by doors painted in oils, is an adaptation of the original design —presented by the Barcelona organ makers Perris Arrabasa and Salvador Estrada in 1561 to the Chapter of Tarragona Cathedral in 1561— by the architect and priest Jaume Amigó who was based in the parish of Tivissa (Tarragona). The sculptural details were carved by Jeroni Sanxo and Perris Ostris, who began work in 1562 and completed the task in 1567. The three sections of the organ are made from Flanders oak, cypress, poplar, elm and yew, and closely follow the stylistic tenets

The organ with its doors closed and open

of the late Renaissance derived from the Plateresque style with recourse to the classical orders, tondos and the characteristic *horror vacui* sculpted with skilful virtuosity. The organ contains an abundance of iconographic motifs: fauna, flora, Atlantis columns, heads of cherubims, human busts, saints, masks, liturgical objects, amphoras and the occasional grotesque figure. An entire ornamental compendium resolved in a beautiful way with a clear educational and moralising intent.

Built in the 16th century, it occupies the left-hand wall of the central nave above a section of the choir stalls

The organ retains the original doors that, when closed, depict the Annunciation of the Archangel Gabriel to the Virgin Mary and, when open, show the mystery of the Nativity and the Resurrection. It also has the serge curtain that covered the organ pipes on the gallery, or *cadireta*, with images of the Virgin Mary, Saint Thecla and Saint Catherine, and the painting in the organ loft depicting the theological virtues: faith, hope and charity. The pictorial ensemble was commissioned by the Cathedral Chapter from the painters Pere Serafí and Pietro Paolo de Montalbergo. Nevertheless, the latter, who hailed from Piedmont, produced all the paintings between 1563 and 1565. The sculptural ensemble on the organ casing was restored in 2012 to return the wood to its natural colour, hidden as a result of a series of unfortunate interventions. Likewise, the four paintings on the doors, the frame, and the opening and closing mechanism were subjected to a delicate and in-depth restoration throughout 2017 and 2018. The pipes of the new Verschueren organ and its musical mechanism, which was fitted in 2013, were adjusted so that it would sound like a 16th- or 17th-century organ. They replaced the early components made by Salvador Estrada in 1567 and the romantic organ donated by Charles Deering in 1917 to Cardinal Francesc d'Assís Vidal Barraquer.

Sculptural details on the *cadireta*

Chapels in the left-hand side nave, or chapels of the Evangelists

Chapel of Saint John the Evangelist

This chapel was begun around 1592 and paid for by Archbishop Joan Terès Borrull (1587-1603). It was completed around 1603. Structurally it is the twin of the chapel of Saint Fructuosus, and was built to plans by the masterly Barcelona architect Pere Blai, who perfectly adapted its layout to the canons established by the classical Renaissance in all its austere magnificence. The understated quality of the chapel is defined by the solidity of its pilasters with their Corinthian capitals,

→ Saint John the Evangelist

arches, ornate cornice placed around the entire perimeter of the chapel, the Corinthian-style portal —which leads into the other chapel—, the flooring with its geometric figures, the bench attached to the plinth around the side walls, and the semi-circular stained-glass window built flush with the surface of the vaulting. All these elements, made of grey stone with a honed finish, highlight and frame the white sections of the vaulting and the central spaces on each wall. The wood reliefs depicting different military outfits and trophies were carved by Benet Baró in 1620 and gilded by Pau Esteve in 1621.

The images worshipped here are those of Saint John the Evangelist, begun by Agustí Bennàsser in 1615 and completed by Baró in 1616. The latter was also commissioned to carve the cypress-wood figures of the holy martyrs Saint Julia and Saint Eulalia of Merida. The gilding and polychrome decoration were done by Francesc Sabater in 1618.

The tomb of Archbishop Terès lies beneath the rounded arch in the wall between this chapel and the adjacent one dedicated to Saint Fructuosus. It consists of a sarcophagus and small temple with a dome and pyramid-shaped finial supported by eight columns. It was made by the master builder Joan Sellimanosa and the sculptor Isaac Alfard Vermey between 1608 and 1610. Improvements were subsequently made to Pere Blai's project by raising the sarcophagus and placing it on a plinth of Tortosa jasper with four white-marble lions on each corner. It was embellished with coats of arms on the sides, volutes at the top, a cross surmounting the finial, and figures alluding to the saints and theological and cardinal virtues sculpted by Agustí Bennàsser in 1613: the ones facing this chapel depict strength, Saint Margaret of Cortona with a dog at her feet, prudence and, probably, Saint Thecla. The temple is reminiscent of the one designed by Bramante in the courtyard of the church of Sant Pietro in Montorio in Rome, and the Patio de los Evangelistas at El Escorial designed by Juan de Herrera.

The sturdy railings around this chapel and the chapels of Saints Fructuosus, Augurius and Eulogius were commissioned by Archbishop Terès from the Barcelona ironsmith Joan Galí and fitted in 1608.

→
Arcosolium and tomb of Archbishop Joan Terès

IOAN TERES CATHALAN. EX CANONICO POENITENTIA
TARRACON. AD ECCLES. MARROH. ELENEN. DERTVSE
AC TARRACON. EVECTVS. PROREGIS. AC CAPITA. GENERAL
CATHALON. OFFICIO FVGENS. TOTIVS PROVICIAE DAMNO
NOBIS ERIPITVR. VI. ID. IVL. M. DCIII. AETA.

Chapel of Saint Fructuosus

This chapel was also an initiative of Archbishop Joan Terès and a result of his devotion to Tarragona's martyr saints. It is Renaissance in style and was begun in 1592 to a design by Pere Blai, and completed in 1603. It is the same as the chapel of Saint John and has a rectangular ground plan, barrel vault reinforced by transverse arches underpinned by pilasters of grey marble-type stone, a semi-circular apse and windows divided into three sections redolent of the classical purity of the Herreran style. The walls are decorated with oils on canvas depicting the chapel's titular saints. They were painted by Hermini Sentís in 1959. The gadroons in the casing of the vault and the ledge under the niches are made of gilded wood with reliefs. The niches house polychrome sculptures of the martyr saints: Bishop Fructuosus and his deacons Augurius and Eulogius who Emperor Valerian condemned to be burnt at the stake in the amphitheatre in Tarragona on 21st January 259 AD. They were carved by Benet Baró in 1616 with gildings and polychrome decorations by Francesc Sabater applied in 1618. The stone altar is separate from the niche in the apse. Steps were added in 1922 along with a white-marble tabernacle for the relics currently housed in the chest inside the cell in the front of the altar.

The burial casket with the recumbent effigy of Archbishop Antolín López Peláez (1913-1918) is attached to the left-hand wall and supported by corbels. It was sculpted in 1920 by the brothers from Barcelona, Llucià and Miquel Oslé Sáenz de Medrano.

The crypt was designed by the architect Manuel Lamic and built in 1978. It houses the tomb of Cardinal Francesc d'Assís Vidal Barraquer (1919-1943) and a stone commemorating his auxiliary bishop, the Blessed Manel Borràs Ferré (1934-1936), flanked by two others listing the diocesan priests martyred during the religious persecutions from 1936 to 1939. They were beatified by the Church on 13th October 2013 in Tarragona and their relics are housed in the silver casket worked by the silversmiths Tena in Barcelona, and in others made of limestone. Bishop Josep Pont Gol (1970-1983) is also buried here.

Chapel crypt

Chapel of the Immaculate Conception

This chapel is a superb example of baroque architecture and consists of a cross-shaped ground plan, semi-spherical central dome and an apsidal chancel. It was built and paid for by Canon Diego Girón de Rebolledo Desplau, who died in 1682, to a project by the Carmelite friar Josep de la Concepció dated 1674. The work was carried out by Magí Costas in collaboration with the father and son team of builders, the Portellas. The chapel is deeper and higher than the others in the cathedral. The rounded arch of the portal leading into the chapel is crowned by the coats of arms of the Rebolledo family. The interior has a Greek-cross ground plan, engaged pilasters, Corinthian capitals, an imposing entablature, a slender semi-spherical dome with a lantern supported by spandrels, a stained-glass windows made by the Barcelona glass artist Francesc Saladrigues in 1682, and a polygonal apse.

→ Chancel and altarpiece

In 1678, while Francesc Grau was carving the altar and magnificent white-marble bench, Domènech Rovira II was working on the imposing Solomonic altarpiece with an enviable attention to detail and a profusion of decorative motifs: the heraldic emblems of the Rebolledo family, panels with reliefs depicting the birth of the Virgin Mary, images of the married saints Joachim and Anna, cherubs, garlands of fruit, canopies, busts of virgins, angels playing musical instruments and depictions of strength, prudence, faith, hope and charity. Josep Cabanyes gilded and polychromed this lavish array of decorative and

Detail of the altarpiece

Statue of the Virgin

iconographic motifs between 1680 and 1684. The statue of the Virgin that is the centre of the altarpiece is by Vicenç Roig Besora (1762-1837). It replaced the original, which was put in storage until 1939, because it wasn't to the liking of the Cathedral Chapter, and subsequently loaned to the parish church of Sant Francesc d'Assis in Tarragona. The sculptors Grau and Rovira II also carved the marble pantheons of Rebolledo and his siblings, which are set into the walls at the sides. Although identical in structure, their sculptural details are different and were painstakingly carved in 1683. The sarcophagus on the left-hand side houses the mortal remains of Diego Girón de Rebolledo decorated with women mourners, images of faith and charity, reliefs alluding to the *Trivium* and *Quadrivium*, as well as an inscription praising the deceased. The one on the right contains the bodies of Joan Godofred and Francesca who were buried, like their brother, in 1684.

→ Sarcophagus of Canon Diego Girón de Rebolledo

The select pictorial repertoire is the work of three noteworthy Catalan artists. Josep Juncosa produced most of the scenes from the life of the Virgin Mary. They are painted in oils on rectangular pieces of twill fabric and hang on the side walls. Saint Diego of Alcalá and Saint Thecla flank the presbytery chancel while other scenes from the life of the Virgin and Christ are depicted inside the respective tondos. Between 1680 and 1684 Juncosa painted different images in tempera that the gilder Josep Cabanyes decorated with figures and phytomorphic motifs between the pilasters, friezes and gadroons in the dome. Francesc Tramulles Roig painted the murals on the intrados of the triumphal arch leading into the chapel, as well as the spandrels, domes, and gadroons in the casing of the apse.

Finally, the ironsmiths from Mataró (Barcelona), Pere Catà and Miquel Esmandia, and the Barcelona-based bronze caster Joan Arnau made the iron and bronze gate that encloses this magnificent chapel dedicated to the Virgin. It dates from 1681 and is an eloquent example of the seamless integration of art and architecture. Catà and Esmandia also cast the vast iron eagle holding up the lamp. It replaced the silver original made by the Barcelona silversmith Bonaventura Fornaguera, which was stolen by the French troops during their calamitous occupation of the cathedral.

Eagle holding the lamp

Chapels of the Cardonas

←
Altarpiece in the chapel of the Virgin of Montserrat

These are two splendid examples of the Florid-Gothic style that, in spite of the occasional nod to the Renaissance, follow the same architectural and ornamental lines: a rectangular ground plan with a single section, a square chancel becoming octagonal at the top with small angular vaults supporting the star-shaped ribbed vault, rounded arches with fringes, phytomorphic and narrative corbels with the Tetramorph, and the heraldic shields of the Cardonas and the Cathedral Chapter, among others. They are the result of the generosity of Archbishop Pere Folch de Cardona (1515-1530) who built them inside his family vault and dedicated them to the Annunciation and Saint Mary Magdalene. The prelate's shield is featured in the respective keystones. Both chapels were built between 1520 and 1525 by the brothers Antoine and Guy Bell-lloch, from Arles (France), who were aided by the stonemason Joan Frexenes de Limoges, and Joan Grau who hailed from Tarragona. The railings around both chapels were forged by the Barcelona ironsmith Josep Carreres in 1715.

Chapel of the Virgin of Montserrat

Although this chapel was previously dedicated to the Annunciation of the Archangel Gabriel to the Virgin Mary, a mystery worshipped in the altarpiece painted by Francesc Olives in the 16th century, it is currently dedicated to the Virgin of Montserrat. There is an incomplete, early-15th century altarpiece in the chancel, above a stone bench. It was placed there in 1932 to replace the original destroyed by Napoleon's troops in 1811. It consists of a series of Gothic panels painted some time between 1403 and 1411 and taken from the old altarpiece from Santes Creus begun by Guerau Gener and complemented by others by Pere Serra and Lluís Borrassà. The scenes with their vibrant colours and delicately rendered figures, depict patriarchs, apostles and saints along the predella. Episodes from the life of the Virgin Mary appear in the side panels. The free-standing polychrome carvings of Saint Benedict of Nursia and Saint Bernard of Clairvaux flank the altarpiece and are attributed to Antoni Canet, who was first recorded in

Detail of the altarpiece

1394. The vault on the left-hand side, which separates this chapel from the chapel of the Cardonas, contains the sumptuous tomb housing the remains of its commissioner, Pere Folch de Cardona. His uncle and aunt, Cardinal Jaume Francesc Folch de Cardona i Gandía, and Timor, abbess of Valldonzella (Barcelona), were also supposed to be interred in the tomb but, despite the laudatory inscriptions about them, they were laid to rest elsewhere and Folch i Cardona's nephew and successor Lluís Folch de Cardona i Enríquez (1531-1532) was buried there instead. The sarcophagus is made of marble decorated with splendid grotesques and, according to some authors, was imported from Italy around 1530. However, others have attributed it to Damián Forment. The sarcophagus on the right, carved by the sculptors Josep Janés and Manuel Roca in 1864, houses the remains of Archbishop Josep Domènec Costa Borràs (1857-1864).

The niche in the centre of the predella houses a sculpture of the Virgin of Montserrat made by Jaume Satorras Capell in the late 20th century.

Chapel of Saint Mary Magdalene

Previously dedicated to Saint Thomas Aquinas, this chapel has the same layout as the chapel of the Annunciation as both were commissioned by the same archbishop and built by the Bell-lloch brothers. The worship of Saint Mary Magdalene was instated in 1334 by Ramon de Ricart, the archdeacon of Vila-seca, in the small shrine, or aedicule, beneath the choir balcony where the statue of Saint Lucy is now worshipped. The Gothic carving of Our Lady of the Pomegranate presides over the altar and Gothic altarpiece. It comes from Alcover (Tarragona) and was made circa 1457.

The arcosolium shared with the chapel of the Annunciation allows us to see the Cardona family vault. On the left-hand wall is the austere sarcophagus of Archbishop Francesc de Fleix Solans (1864-1875), carved by Agapit Vallmitjana Barbany in 1879.

In 1864, Archbishop Josep Domènec Costa Borràs hired the Tarragona-born painter Miquel Fluixenc to do a painting featuring the episode of the Annunciation to be hung in the chapel. This painting was moved to the chapel of the Virgin of the Cloisters, where it is currently worshipped, when the new altar and altarpiece were built and dedicated in 1856.

Arcosolium
and sarcophagus
of the Cardonas

IACOBO·ACARDONA CARDINALI
DIGNISSIMO·PETRVS·ARCHIEPVS·
TARACONENSIS·REGIVSQ3·CANC
ELLARIVS·NEPOS·ET·ALVMNVS
STATVENDVM·CVRAVIT

Chapels in the left retrochoir, or chapels of the Evangelist

The spaces between the four intercolumns, leading off the central nave and outside the walls of the choir, house a series of chapels. They have been dedicated to different saints over the years.

Chapel of Saint Elizabeth, or chapel of the Dormition of the Virgin

There are records of a chapel and low altar dedicated to Saint Elizabeth of Hungary, commissioned in her memory in 1251 by her sister, Queen Violant (1216-1251), the wife of King Jaime I of Aragon (1208-1276). The altar was consecrated by papal bull in 1259. The walls with their polychrome decorations are the only original features of the chapel to survive. The basket arch, false wooden ceiling and the door to the spiral staircase leading to the old organ console date from the 16th century. Highlights include the series of pictorial motifs uncovered on the ashlars in 2012 that have been dated to the third or fourth decade of the 14th century. Equally noteworthy are a trompe l'oeil tapestry with a rhomboid trim containing gammadion crosses and, on its left, the bust of two angels flying above a recumbent female figure, who may represent the Dormition of the Virgin or Saint Elizabeth herself, and the continuous frieze with alternating floral panels and heraldic emblems referring to the Cathedral Chapter, the Crown of Aragon and dynasties of the canons.

The clothed effigy of the Dormition of the Virgin, recumbent inside the casket, was carved in 1771 by Carles Grau, an architect and sculptor from Barcelona. It was paid for by the canon and hospitaller Francesc Xavier Foguet Aldomar and was part of the catafalque of the Mystery of the Dormition of the Virgin, destroyed between 1937 and 1939.

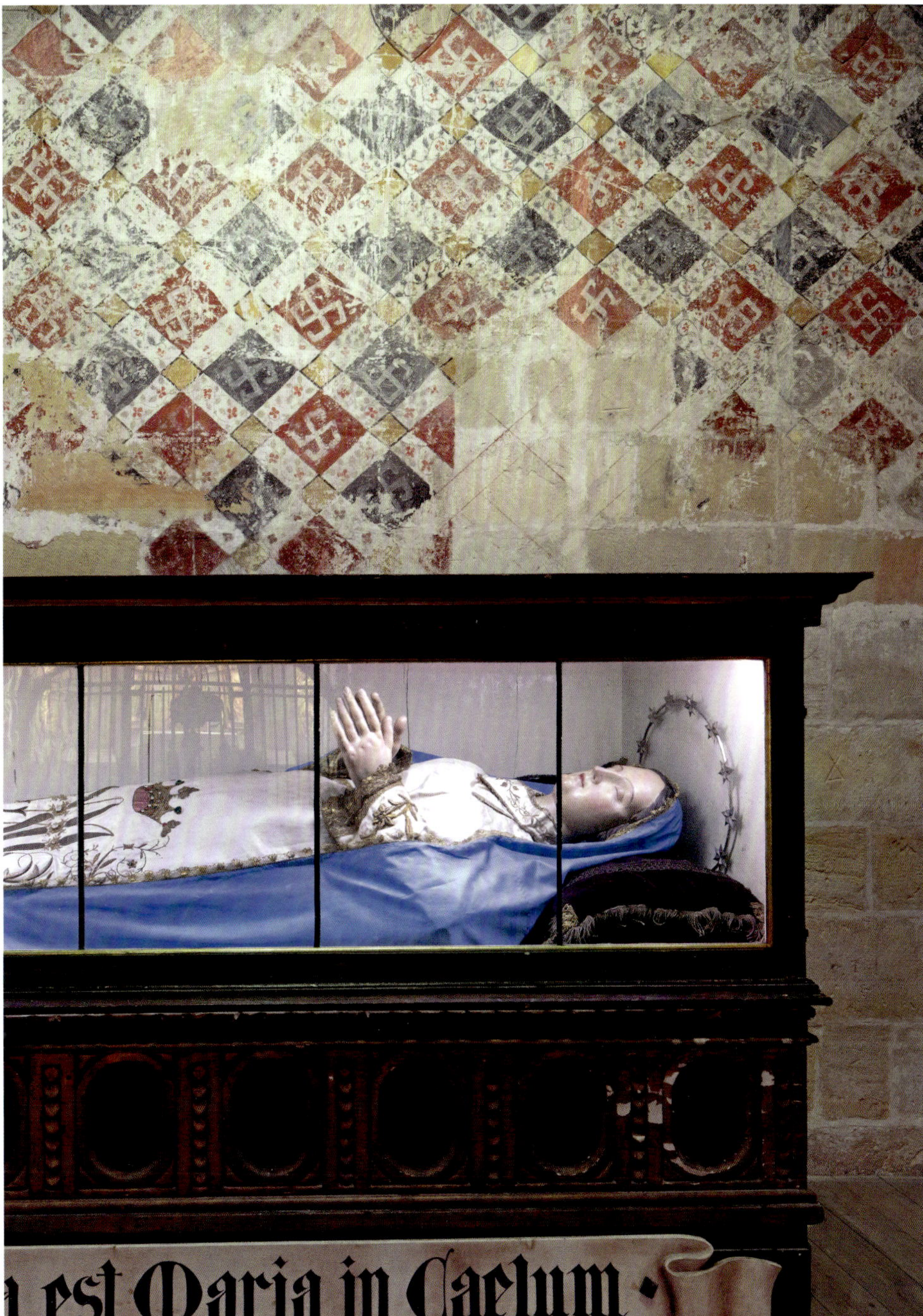

Effigy of the Dormition of the Virgin and murals

Chapel of the Holy Sepulchre

This unique chapel was built between 1494 and 1511 in the Flamboyant-Gothic style. The twin entrance is composed of two ogee arches with floral finials, leaf decorations on the extrados, together with the emblems of the Cathedral Chapter and the canon and promoter of the chapel Joan Barceló on the intrados. The entrance is framed by basket arches flanked by stylised columns resembling spires and lavishly decorated with fantastic fauna, masks and leaf motifs. In 1328, the canon Jofre de Cruïlles dedicated this aedicule to Saint Volusian, bishop of Tours. The saint was worshipped at the Gothic altarpiece put in place around 1332 and the centrepiece of the chapel until the devotion to Christ in the sepulchre was introduced in 1496. The 4th-century Roman marble sarcophagus containing the recumbent effigy of Christ is surrounded by a series of polychrome limestone figures from the scene of the Holy Burial. They are the work of an anonymous Valencian sculptor and represent the Virgin Mary, Mary Magdalene, Mary Salome, Saint John the Evangelist, Joseph of Arimathea and Nicodemus. The central panel of the sarcophagus, flanked by strigils, reproduces the narrative shield of the founder bearing the inscription "Lord, grant the doors of salvation until the end of days / MCCCCLXXXXIIII". It is made of polychrome stone and was inlaid in 1494.

→
Entrance and vault of the chapel

In the 17th century, Francesc Sabater gilded and coloured the spaces between the mouldings of the ribbed vault decorated with curling flower leaves *a candelieri*, the heads of angels and the *Arma Christi* and instruments of the Passion stemming from the mannerist repertoire.

The keystone contains the Gothic trigram of Christ. Furnished only the sarcophagus containing the effigy of the dead Christ, the chapel invites reflection, silence and prayer.

Emblem of Joan Barceló

Chapels in the right-hand side nave, or chapels of the Epistle

Chapel of Saint Ursula and the Eleven Thousand Virgins, or chapel of the Baptistry

The chapel was built between 1335 and 1340 under the patronage of Archbishop Arnau de Sescomes (1335-1346) and dedicated to Saint Ursula and the Eleven Thousand Virgins. The archbishop's burial slab is set into the floor. The chapel is Gothic in style and has a polygonal chancel, stylised twin stained-glass windows with richly foiled tracery, a star vault and notable reliefs bearing the image of Saint Michael on the transverse arch; the Coronation of the Virgin, and Saint Paul and Saint Thecla on the main keystones; and busts of virgin saints wearing crowns on the smaller keystones. A number of free-standing sculptures and frescoes with the heads of the dedicatee saints, discovered beneath the whitewash, are all that survive from the original decorations. Archbishop Juan of Aragon (1328-1334) donated Saint Ursula's skull to the cathedral —hence the name of the chapel— together with other relics from the maidens who were martyred with her. The number of maidens has been misconstrued over the years due to the fact that the acronym XI.V.M. has been interpreted as "eleven thousand virgins" rather than "eleven virgin martyrs". The central window retains a section of the original 14th-century stained-glass windows. The polychrome decoration of the figurative tapestry on the right-hand wall at the chapel entrance, and the corresponding capital, were discovered in 2012. The original altar and effigies of the virgins suffered the effects of the Napoleonic invasion and this is why the spartan chapel was converted into the baptistry in 1821 as a result of a donation from Canon Bernardí Llopis Fiats. It was decorated with the relief of the Baptism

→
Sarcophagus of Cardinal Gaspar Cervantes de Gaeta

←
Baptismal font

of Christ carved by Vicenç Roig Besora in 1835, and the monumental baptismal font made from one of the blocks that were originally part of the frieze from the temple of Augustus that was renovated during the reign of Emperor Hadrian (117-138) using white marble from the island of Proconnesus (Bosporus). The aforementioned relief is currently housed in the cloister chapel of Saint Salvador. When the chapel was restored in 1932, it was decorated with sculptures of the virgins that had been dispersed in different areas of the cathedral.

The wall separating this chapel from the chapel of Saint Michael was cleared in the late 16th century as stipulated in the will of Cardinal Gaspar Cervantes de Gaeta (1568-1575) to house his tomb in a similar manner to the Cardonas', although he specified that he wanted it to be less ornate. The tomb was designed by Jaume Amigó in 1575 and consists of three sections decorated with laudatory epitaphs, the bishop's emblem edged by two *putti* lamenting on the back, the sculptures of strength, Saint Mary Magdalene and the Virgin Mary (?) that weren't originally intended for the mausoleum. The ensemble is surmounted by the figure of Charity.

The arcosolium on the right-hand wall houses the tomb of the cardinal-archbishop Manuel Arce Ochotorena (1944-1948) made in 1952. The wrought-iron railings were made by an ironsmith from Morella (Castellón) in 1438. They were taken from the ancient presbytery restored in 1963 and funded by the canon and archdeacon from Vila-seca, Pere Ramon. The central panel and the decorations of the finial with gilded applications date from 1599 and are by Agustí Mallorquí.

Chapel of Saint Michael

All that survives from the original chapel is its Gothic structure with its polygonal ground plan, the star ribbed vault decorated with magnificent keystones, corbels and cornices sculpted with angels playing musical instruments and the evangelists Matthew, Mark, Luke and John. It was built as a result of the generosity of Guillem Bonsoms, the archdeacon of the church of Sant Llorenç, begun around 1365 and completed around 1379. The Virgin and Child are depicted on the transverse arch and the *Maiestas Domini* and Saint Michael feature on the keystones. The paintings on the right-hand wall resemble stained-glass windows. They date from the late 15th century and feature an angel, Saint Agnes and Saint Bartholomew. The dean Joan de Montoliu i de Boixadors obtained permission from the Chapter in 1770 to replace the early Gothic stone altar with an altarpiece dedicated to Saint Michael the Archangel, a monumental polychrome carving that survives today. It was made by the sculptor Antoni Pallàs between 1767 and 1770. The stained-glass windows in the chancel were created by Jeroni Granell in 1958. It was around this time that the Saint Michael altarpiece was placed behind the altar. It is painted in tempera on board with gilded decorations and is an example of the International Gothic style. The altarpiece is attributed to Bernat Martorell and comes from the parish church of La Pobla de Cérvoles (Lleida). It is dated circa 1435. The predella contains scenes from the Passion of Christ, the central panel shows Saint Michael brandishing his lance at a dragon, and the top contains a Calvary. The side panels feature scenes associated with the fight between good and evil.

→ Saint Michael altarpiece

The blocked-up Gothic door on the left-hand wall used to be called "del Fillols" (the godchildren's), because it was used by novice monks to enter the ancient baptistry that stood on the site currently occupied by the chapel of Saint Thecla. The wall on the left-hand side was cleared to replicate architecturally the Roman-style portal in the chapel of Saint Ursula, or the chapel of the Baptistry, whose arcosolium holds the sarcophagus of Archbishop Gaspar Cervantes de Gaeta (1568-1575).

The chapel is enclosed by a wrought-iron railing with floral finials inset with the Tau of the Chapter and the tip of a lance.

Chapel of Saint Thecla

The cathedral is dedicated to Saint Thecla, the patron saint of Tarragona. When the relic of the saint's arm was brought to the cathedral, a silver reliquary, now missing, was produced during the tenure of Archbishop Juan of Aragon (1328-1334) together with the painted altarpiece dedicated to the saint in the apsidiole of the side nave on the right. Archbishop Manuel de Samaniego Jaca (1722-1744) commissioned a sumptuous chapel, the last one to be built in the cathedral, to further highlight the local community's devotion to the protomartyr from Iconium who is worshipped at the altarpiece above the high altar. The archbishop's successor, Jaume de Cortada i de Brú (1753-1762), laid the first stone of the chapel on 17th August 1760, on the site occupied by the ancient baptistry. The chapel was completed in 1775 when Juan Lario Lancis (1764-1777) was archbishop. The architectural and sculptural ensemble is predominantly classical-baroque in style, remaining faithful to the academic tenets of the day, advocated by Louis XV. This sumptuous structure was designed by Josep Prat Delorta with a Greek-cross ground plan and a large dome underpinned by spandrels, decorated with locally quarried jasper, fine marble, reliefs, sculptures, floral garlands and cherubims. There is a white-marble high relief above the chancel depicting a cloud of glory around the saint in ecstasy before the Mystic Lamb. At its feet, is the gilded bronze door of the niche containing the ebony and silver casket carved by Sebastià Picanyol in 1817. The casket contains the relic of the Holy Arm that King Ixion of Cilician Armenia gave to Jaime II of Aragon in 1321. The figure of the lion and bear stand guard at the sides of the casket, symbols of hope in the resurrection. The iconographic programme is completed with busts of Saint Basil (?-458/460) and Saint John Chrysostom (344/354-407), who wrote the history of Saint Thecla.

The casket contains the relic of the Holy Arm that King Ixion of Cilician Armenia gave to Jaime II of Aragon in 1321

The original reliquary was stolen by the French troops when they laid siege to the cathedral. The current one, in the shape of a clothed forearm and hand, is attributed

Arm reliquary

Saint Thecla altarpiece

Detail of the transverse arch in the chapel

The Four Cardinal Virtues

to the Barcelona silversmith Francesc Pintó Valls. It was made in the same year as the silver casket and the purity of the silver is shown by the hallmark of Josep Rovira. Two niches in the cornerstones of the dome house female figures symbolising the Four Cardinal Virtues: prudence, justice, fortitude and temperance. The high reliefs on the side walls, depicting Saint Thecla visiting Saint Paul in prison and the martyrdom of the flames, are made of plaster of Paris. The central relief, showing the glorification of Saint Thecla, and the lavish ornamental repertoire by Carles Sala, are clearly influenced by Gian Lorenzo Bernini (1598-1680). The pink Tortosa jasper and white Carrara marble ennoble the chapel bathed in iridescent light from the original Murano glass lamps and enclosed by interesting railings forged by Onofre Camps.

Detail of the door to the niche that houses the reliquary

Chapel of Saint Francis of Assisi

This simple and austere Renaissance chapel has a semi-circular transverse arch with square panels on the intrados, a cornice, two stretches of ribbed vaulting, a polygonal apse with a gadrooned casing, and end windows crowned by bullseyes with stained-glass windows. It was built between 1580 and 1584 to a project by the architect and priest Jaume Amigó at the behest of the dean Lluís-Gabriel Robuster Nebot, who received financial assistance from the merchant Gabriel Nebot, a relative of his. The altarpiece is in the mannerist style and was made in the 17th century. It is decorated with Corinthian columns and strings of fruit and has as its centrepiece a painting of Saint Francis of Assisi receiving the stigmata, attributed to Josep Juncosa. Two vast oil paintings done by the Genovese artist Giacomo Giustiniano around 1625 hang on the side walls. They were paid for by Canon Vicenç Tarragó, prior of the cathedral's Community of Presbyters. They depict the *Massacre of the Innocents* ordered by Herod, and the *Adoration of the Kings*. The latter is attributed to the painter's daughter Angélica.

The arcosolium in the left wall houses the sarcophagus with the mortal remains of Canon Cristòfol Robuster Tarragó i de Samant, a relative of Nebot's, who obtained permission from the Cathedral Chapter to build the tomb and be buried there.

The chapel is enclosed by simple wrought-iron railings made in the middle of the 19th century and paid for by Archbishop Josep Domènec Costa Borràs (1857-1864).

→
Altarpiece with the image of Saint Francis of Assisi

Sarcophagus of Canon Cristòfol Robuster Tarragó i de Samant

IHS MRA

Chapel of the Presentation of Jesus at the Temple

This is the oldest of the cathedral chapels. It is open fronted and was built between the buttresses in the late 13th or early 14th centuries. The epitaph to the dean Dalmau de Montoliu, who died in 1306 and is buried in the chapel, attests to this. The portal has a rounded arch replacing the pointed one, and is decorated with mouldings and blind arches. The simple, square ground plan is covered by a ribbed vault in four sections and a keystone with a carved image of the Lamb of God, an image that suggests an early devotion to the Saviour. The stone lintel above one of the doors leading into the sacristy suggests the chapel was altered during the Renaissance. The high relief of the altarpiece, depicting the Presentation of Jesus at the temple and the Purification of the Virgin Mary, was carved and left blank by Vicenç Roig Besora (1762/64-1837) some time between the late 18th and early 19th centuries. About a hundred years later, possibly in the middle of the 20th century, the Tarragona-born painter, Sadurní García Anguera (1912-1963) polychromed the altarpiece. The current altar was dedicated and blessed by Cardinal Archbishop Benjamín de Arriba y Castro (1948-1970). It was remodelled in 2007 to accommodate the liturgical reforms of the 2nd Vatican Council. Bakers' utensils and ears of wheat decorating the columns of the *mensa* remind us that the Guild of Bakers worshipped in this chapel from the 16th century onwards.

The polychrome wood oval reliefs above the lintels of the side doors were part of the altarpiece in the chapel of Saint Olegarius carved by Francesc Bonifàç in 1776. The one on the left portrays Saint John the Baptist and Saint John the Evangelist; and the one on the right, Saint Paul and Saint Thecla. On the left wall we find the funerary stele with a relief of Calvary and a text in praise of the dean Dalmau de Montoliu.

The iron railings were made in the middle of the 19th century and paid for by Archbishop Josep Domènec Costa Borràs (1857-1864).

Relief of Saint Paul and Saint Thecla

Chapels in the right retrochoir, or chapels of the Epistle

The most important series of proto-Gothic murals is found in the chapels in the retrochoir on the side of the chapels of the Epistle. The Italo-Gothic-style figures of the saints are depicted in a frontal, hieratic pose and set into vertical compartments. They were discovered by chance under a layer of whitewash in 1933 and are dated between 1330 and 1350. They are attributed to the same artist.

Chapel of Saint Helena

The chapel has no vault and its chancel is the wall enclosing the former choir bounded by a cornice and with canonical elements. Formerly known as the chapel of the souls, it was dedicated to the worship of

Saint Blaise, Saint Apollonia, Saint Agnes and Saint Marina. It was subsequently dedicated to Saint Roch and Saint Sebastian. In 1933 —following the removal of the altarpiece and altar of the souls and a niche placed there in 1879, paid for by a parishioner and containing a statue of Saint Lucy— images of the saints and episodes referring to the Quest for the True Cross of Christ on the rocky outcrop of Golgotha in Jerusalem in 326 AD were revealed. The central composition is divided into two sections depicting the discovery of the cross. A group of Jews, who are identified by the white cockade on their clothing, had hidden it in a water tank where it was discovered by the servants of Saint Helena, the mother of Emperor Constantine, who is seen devoutly worshipping the holy cross. These scenes are flanked by the figures of the following saints: Anthony the Abbot with the devil at his feet, Helena holding the Crown of Thorns, Felix of Scilitana, and Alexius.

At the top of the right-hand column, on a ledge, stands the equestrian figure of Saint Hippolytus healing a man's throat. This polychrome stone figure dates from 1405, and was donated by Ferrer Pi. It was taken from the chapel of Saint John and placed here in 1605. The railings around the chapel, and the adjacent one of Saint Lucy, were made at the behest of Archbishop Pedro de Urrea (1445-1489).

Murals: Saint Helena, Quest for the True Cross and Saint Felix

Chapel of Saint Lucy

This is a tiny chapel, just like the other ones housed in the intercolumns around the stalls in the former choir. It consists of a wall and columns that mark out the first section of the nave of the Epistle. The chapel was built in the 14th century and dedicated to Saint Mary Magdalene. It was funded by the prebend instated by the archdeacon of Vila-seca, Ramon de Ricart, in 1334. The moulded segmental arch was built in the 16th century, along with the wooden ceiling, balustrade and spiral staircase leading to the upper gallery. Saint Fabian and Saint Sebastian were also worshipped in this chapel, as attested to by a painting of the saints donated by the priest Josep Solanelles in 1782 and placed above the altar. It was replaced by a neoclassical wooden altarpiece with a statue of the Virgin of Montserrat donated in 1831 by one of the cathedral's beneficiaries, Anton Ràfols Fernández. When the altarpiece was dismantled in 1935 to be moved to the chapel of Saint Michael (La Pobla de Cérvoles, Lleida), frescoes were uncovered with images of Saint Narcissus wearing pontifical vestments, and Saint Martha of Bethany with the fearsome dragon, the tarasque, at her feet. She is holding a book open at a page containing an incomplete verse from the Requiem Mass. The polychrome statue of Saint Lucy was placed there in 1941. It was made around 1879 by an unknown sculptor. During restoration work in 2012, the staircase leading to the upper gallery was removed and a third figure was revealed who may be the martyr Saint Valerian. On the left-hand side, halfway down the wall, we see the head of Saint Maximus, bishop of Aix-en-Provence (France).

These frescoes, like the ones in the chapel of Saint Helena, have been attributed to the same anonymous artist who painted them during the third or fourth decade of the 14th century, a period when the worship of the True Cross, the Holy Thorn and the Body of Christ had become a central part of religious ceremonies at the cathedral.

Fresco: Saint Narcissus, Saint Martha of Bethany and Saint Valerian (?)

Cloisters

It would appear that the cloisters were begun at the same time as the cathedral because of the heraldic castles and rocks on some of the imposts in the northern corner and others in the centre of the north-west wing, attributable to Archbishop Ramon de Castellterçol (1194-1198) and his successor Ramon de Rocabertí (1199-1215). This hypothesis is supported by a contract drawn up by the prelate in 1214 concerning the building of the cloisters to which he bequeathed a large sum of money. These details confirm that the work commenced in the late 12th century and was completed during the second half of the 13th century.

← North-west gallery

The cloisters were a place for reading, walking and meditation, suitable for processions and the site of the main communal areas used by the members of the clergy: the chapter house, church, refectory, library and dormitory. They are situated on the corner formed by the left arm of the cathedral transept and chancel. The north-west and north-east galleries are aligned with the walls of the imposing Temenos, an enclosure built during the rule of the Flavian dynasty in the 1st century AD and later used as the site for the cathedral and canons' chambers. The walls are not the only elements that attest to the presence of the Romans in the cloisters. The marble reused to build the columns and Romanesque portal, the ashlars with their inscriptions, and the remains of a frieze with bucranes may originally have been part of the temple of Augustus. The discovery of the foundations of the exedra in the north-west section of the Imperial place of worship provide further evidence of Roman occupation of the site. It is reached from the cloisters and has a sturdy rounded arch inside that was once part of the original entrance to this aedicule.

The cloisters contain some two hundred and ninety-five white-marble capitals and imposts

The mullion and door leading into the cloisters

The cloisters were built to a square, slightly irregular (47 × 46 m) ground plan. They have ribbed vaults with simple mouldings, corbels carved with different motifs, and interesting keystones

Galleries of the cloisters

Capitals in the cloisters. Below, cymatium with the *Procession of the rats*.

associated with the early-Gothic style. Each of the four galleries is divided into six sections containing a load-bearing pointed arch beneath which there are two small Islamic-style porthole windows with lattice tracery and three rounded arches resting on twin columns. Inside the gallery each section is divided by sturdy abutments clad in two marble half columns. The outer side of the abutments is faced with a slender limestone column with a Corinthian-style capital. The abutments underpin the cornice on the outside, interrupting the frieze of multifoil blind arches that surmount the frontispiece of the galleries.

The cloisters contain some two hundred and ninety-five white-marble capitals and imposts. Twenty-eight of them are carved with an evocative variety of narrative scenes. Halfway along the south-east wing we see Adam and Eve, Cain and Abel, Abraham with his son Isaac, and Joseph. The corners of the north-west and north-east wings show scenes from the life of Noah, the Passion of Christ, the banquet of the rich man Epulon, the offerings of Cain and Abel, and the death of Abel. In the centre of the north-west wing are scenes from the Resurrection of Christ and the battles of Samson and a Christian knight with a lion. Worthy of mention in the southernmost section of the wing are the cycles of the childhood of Christ and his public life, scenes from the life of Saint Nicholas of Bari and a peculiar calendar showing the months of the year. The remaining capitals are decorated with palm leaves, geometric figures, monsters, fantastic beasts and fables, including the famous *Procession of the rats*. The frieze shows the rodents carrying a cat on a pole. The animal plays dead and attacks by surprise the bearers who are taking it for burial. This scene can be found on a cymatium in the south-east wing and is inspired by an allegory in the *Physiologus*, the most famous medieval bestiary.

Fragments of the ornamental friezes taken from Roman ruins, and the last will and testament of Berenguer de Puigverd dated 1297, were set into the south-west wall to mark the visit to Tarragona of Prince Fernando of Bourbon and his wife Maria Josepha Amalia of Saxony. The floor was laid in 1932 with the thick stone paving slabs used in the city's pavements. They replaced the original earthenware tiles. The four galleries enclose a landscaped area, the *hortus conclusus*, which evokes the lost earthly paradise with its plants and fountains.

Door to the cloisters

← Romanesque portal

Below, detail of the tympanum

This magnificent, austere Romanesque portal, carved from white marble some time between 1200 and 1230, leads from the cloisters into the cathedral. Its size and proportions suggest it was purpose-built for this site and not as an entrance to the cathedral. Nevertheless, it appears to have been made before the cloisters were built. It comprises three concentric archivolts supported by jamb shafts and framing the tympanum that houses the hieratic *Maiestas Domini*, edged by the mandorla and in the company of the tetramorph, or symbols of the evangelists Matthew (Angel), Mark (Lion) Luke (Ox) and John (Eagle). The base of the mullion is decorated with serpents, the symbol of sin and death, and the capital features scenes of the Nativity of Christ, the Magi before Herod and Herodias, and the Epiphany. The scenes are separated by slender columns and the arches crowned by angel acolytes and turrets representing the heavenly Jerusalem. The capitals at the sides feature flora and fauna reminiscent of the classical style. The first capital in the group on the left features the Magi who are lying on the same bed listening in dreams to the warning of the angel. Another capital on the right features a scene with the empty tomb and the Holy Shroud, and the soldiers and the angel announcing the Resurrection of Christ to Mary Magdalene, Mary Clopas and Mary Salome.

The portal is stamped with the chrismon, or monogram of Christ, with the letters alpha and omega, that allude to the Redeemer as the beginning and end of all Creation.

Capital on the mullion: Nativity and Epiphany (detail)

Gardens in the north-west wing of the cloisters

Panoramic view of the cloisters
and cathedral

Gardens in the cloisters

Chapels in the cloisters

According to the *Llibre de Visites Pastorals* of 1449, written during the tenure of Archbishop Pedro de Urrea (1445-1489), there were only three chapels inside the cloisters until the 15th century: the chapel of Saint Anne and Saint Bernard; the chapel of Saint Mary and Saint Simeon; and the chapel of Corpus Christi.

Chapel of Our Lady of the Snows

A Gothic chapel built around 1414 and furnished in the early 1430s by Pere de Vallfogona, the master builder at the cathedral, with the help of the quarrymen Guillem de Camprodon and Guillem de la Mota. It was paid for by Pere Poch, who hailed from Tarragona and is buried here. Until 1630 the chapel was dedicated solely to Saint Bernard who was worshipped at an altarpiece later replaced by another with images of Saint Joachim, Saint Anna and Saint Bernard. It has a noteworthy portal with mouldings decorated with leaf motifs on the extrados, a narrow initial section with a ribbed vault and three keystones. The one in the centre of the transverse arch depicts Saint Thecla; the one above the first vault features the Tau of the Cathedral Chapter; and the second features the Virgin and the Christ Child. Equally noteworthy is the ornate chancel with its radial ribs flanked by leaves resting on corbels carved with motifs and fantastic fauna. The walls are dotted with the emblems of the promoters and the Cathedral Chapter. An oil painting by an unknown artist hangs above the altar. It shows Our Lady of the Snows, or Good News, and was painted in 1705. It is a free interpretation of the icon worshipped at the church of Santa Maria del Popolo in Rome. The railings were made in 1414 by Vidal Gassia, an ironsmith from Tarragona.

→ Chapel of Our Lady of the Snows

High relief of the Baptism of Christ in the chapel of Saint Salvador

Chapel of Saint Salvador

A Renaissance chapel built at the behest of Nicolau Albanell and his wife Ángela Trillo with permission being granted by the Cathedral Chapter in 1533. The chapel was dedicated and blessed on 11th April 1535. It is built of limestone and has a square ground plan that adheres closely to the basic tenets of the Renaissance: a rounded arch around the door with ribs set into the intrados and a generous barrel vault with square panels over a continuous frieze of triglyphs and metopes. The altar was built by the beneficiary Pere Mir in 1537. A painting of Christ was placed above the altar and replaced at a later date by another depicting Saint Thecla. The current altarpiece features a high relief of the baptism of Christ that has

been displayed on the frontal since 1932. It was carved around 1835 by Vicenç Roig Besora and is made of pine with white stucco-work. It was taken from the chapel of the Baptistry and replaced another dedicated to Our Lady of Hope dated 1537.

Chapel of Our Lady of the Cloister

The first records of a chapel dedicated to Our Lady of the Cloister date from 1327. Nevertheless, people had begun worshipping her before this time inside a canonical chapel where the sacristy now stands. In 1514, the canon and hospitaller Francesc de Soldevila wanted to build a chapel. However, his plan never came to fruition because, in 1520, Luis Muñoz, canon and archdeacon of the church of Sant Llorenç, obtained permission from the Cathedral Chapter to build his own chapel and be buried there alongside his relatives. The exterior Gothic portal, jambs and capitals are part of this early structure. The first chapel was demolished between 1674 and 1680, for reasons unknown, and a new one built on the same site. The new chapel was bigger and adopted a Greek-cross ground plan with a central dome. During building work, the statue of Our Lady of the Cloister was transferred to the chapel of Corpus Christi. The rebuilding work was paid for by local worshippers and by the Archbishop Juan Manuel de Espinosa (1664-1679).

During the Napoleonic siege of the city in 1811, a bomb destroyed the original dome, the altarpiece and altar. The statue of Our Lady survived and was transferred to the Tailors' chapel. From 1814 onwards, when the city had already been liberated from the French troops, the Cathedral Chapter embarked on the third and final reconstruction phase of the chapel that lasted until 1852. The cruciform ground plan was restored with its central dome and eight pilasters embedded into the corner abutments at the crossing of the transept. They provide support for the cornice, which forms the base of the transverse arches on which the drum underpinning the dome rests. Four rectangular leaded stained-glass windows filter the light that enters the chapel.

The main building work concluded in 1856 with the current marble altar and altarpiece based on the classicist design by the Tarragona-born sculptor Bernat Verderol. The bases of the columns feature phytomorphic motifs and noteworthy reliefs alluding to the litanies of the Virgin Mary. The chamber above the altar had to be rebuilt in 1913 and 1915 due to water leaks and the classicist design was lost. A new art-nouveau-style ornamental design and layout were adopted, under the supervision of the chapel administrator, Canon Josep Caixal Estradé. The carpentry work was assigned to Josep Verderol, the stonework to Joan Alemany, and the gilding to Antoni Sanahuja. From 1915 to 1920 new improvements were made to the chamber above the altar and presbytery and paid for by the Cathedral Chapter. The project was planned and supervised by the diocesan architect Ramon Salas

→
Chapel dome

Ricomà with the help of experts and the gilder Ferreté who did the stucco and sgraffito work.

This tiny chamber houses the polychrome sculpture of Our Lady of the Cloister. It is made of wood and dates from the late 13th or early 14th centuries. She is seated and dressed in a rose-coloured tunic, blue mantle, white veil and is suckling her son who is wrapped in a shawl, long shirt and vest. They are both wearing crowns made in the 20th century. No traces of the original polychrome work or gilding survive because the effigy suffered damage over the centuries. It was restored in 1911 on the occasion of its canonical coronation during the tenure of Archbishop Tomàs Costa Fornaguera (1889-1911).

← Chamber above the altar with the statue of Our Lady of the Cloister

A canvas with a scene from the Annunciation hangs on the left wall. It was painted by the Tarragona-born artist Miquel Fluixenc Trill in 1864. The remaining paintings, dated from the 17th to 18th centuries, show the Apparition of the Virgin to Saint Francis of Paula and Saint Philip Neri. A pipe organ donated by a group of worshippers in 1700 stands above the choir. After going through the cloister railings —fitted in 1915 and attributed to the ironsmith Ramón Almenara— you can see the tombs of Archbishop Antonio Fernando de Echánove Zaldívar (1825-1854) and Vicenç Falconer, physician to the Cathedral Chapter who died in 1693.

Chapel chancel

Chapel of Our Lady of Guidance

This Gothic-style chapel was built by the cathedral prior, Canon Bertràn de Montoliu, and his brother, Vice-Admiral Berenguer. This is borne out by their crest that decorates the keystone in the centre of the ribbed vault and the donations, or prebends, they introduced between 1293 and 1323. The chapel was built around 1300 to accommodate the gigantic polychrome carving of the saint housed in the niche in the chancel. The carving is one of the oldest in the cathedral and has been recorded in documents under its nickname *La Grossa* (The Big One). It is the only outstanding artwork in the chapel. Mother and child are crudely depicted in out-of-scale proportions and wear hieratic expressions. The Virgin's head and back of her shoulders are carved from pine. The head and feet of the Christ Child, his hands and the Virgin's, are also made from polychrome wood. The rest of the statue is made from plaster mixed with glue and overlaid with twill. The mounting and technique of this *Deiparae*, which was retouched during the baroque era, hark back chronologically to the 13th and 14th centuries. The altar table rests on a drum in the form of a Roman column.

The wrought-iron railings around the chapel were placed there in 1892 to replace the original wooden ones.

Sculpture of Our Lady of Guidance

Chapel of Saint Mary Magdalene

The chapel was built with a donation from the merchant Arnau Balle in 1536. It is Plateresque in style, lavishly decorated and has a rectangular ground plan. The intrados of the transverse arch at the entrance and the side pilasters are decorated with grotesque motifs *a candelieri*. The keystone above the portal is embellished with the Balles family's heraldic emblem and, above it, a free-standing statue of Mary Magdalene accompanied by the heads of cherubims and basilisks as guardians of paradise. The artistic Plateresque railings adorned with chimeras, the trigram of Christ, sphinxes, volutes and tetrapetalous flowers, are one of the few surviving examples of 16th-century Catalan ironwork with this structure and design. The interior is covered by a barrel vault with

→ Saint Mary Magdalene altarpiece

square panels framing rosettes, resting on a perimetral frieze of triglyphs and metopes bearing the family crests of the commissioners and the Cathedral Chapter. A stone bench decorated at the base with a series of triglyphs and metopes encircles the perimeter of the floor divided on the back wall to encompass the altar. The altarpiece contains an image of Saint Mary Magdalene in the centre accompanied by other panels with scenes from her life. It is attributed to Francesc Olives and may have been painted around 1536.

Chapel of Saint Raymond

→
Narrative keystones on the vaulting

It was built in 1520 and funded by Canon Joan Poblet. Originally devoted to Our Lady of Piety, in the 19th century the chapel was rededicated to Saint Raymond. It is late Gothic in design and has a polygonal ground plan. It retains part of the original floor made of glazed blue slabs. The ogee arch around the portico with concentric arches and tracery on the intrados, the small initial stretch of the ribbed vault, the three voluminous keystones carved with images of Saint Catherine of Alexandria, and the emblem of the founder and Saint John the Baptist that still have some of the original polychrome work, have been meticulously executed. Equally splendid is the groin vault with radial mouldings resting on capitals underpinned by engaged half columns. The carvings on the corbels are of excellent quality and great expressive power: lions holding in their claws the founder's heraldic device, the skull referring to death, and the Tetramorph with its respective zoomorphic symbols holding the phylacteries. The sculpture that is the centrepiece of the chapel is by the Reus-born sculptor Ramon Ferran Pagés, and was carved from marble resin in 1989 at the request of the archbishop of Tarragona, Ramon Torrella Cascante (1983-1997). The archbishop's tombstone is set into the floor next to the chapel founder's. The wrought-iron railings were paid for by Canon Joan Coromines and fitted in 1894 as a replacement for the original wooden ones.

Chapel of Saint Raymond

Chapel of Corpus Christi

The chapel was once used as the cathedral chapter house. The door with its rounded arch, flanked by two twin windows with marble frames is the epitome of monastic architecture. The hall, with its square ground plan, pointed barrel vault and a section of a Roman wall at its base, was built at the start of the 13th century. Following a meeting of the canons in the hall of the chapterhouse archive, Archbishop Juan of Aragón (1328-1334) accepted a request from the provost Guerau de Rocabertí and his sister, the widow of Guerau Alemany, to demolish the end wall and build a chapel in the form of a polygonal apse dedicated to the worship of the Eucharist and where its founders could be buried. The chapel was built in 1330 and has been known ever since as the chapel of Corpus Christi. The polychrome relief on the keystone shows an exceptional attention to detail and depicts Christ in Majesty showing the Blessed Sacrament and holding the Gospels. As part of the conversion, the side walls of the Gothic chancel were decorated with images of the Annunciation of the Archangel Gabriel to the Virgin Mary, and the Romanesque walls in the nave were embellished with a series of saints and apostles carved in stone with their respective phylacteries. They were sculpted in the first half of the 14th century and contain traces of the original polychrome work, as well as the emblems of Gerau de Rocabertí along the walls of the apse and gadroons in the vault.

The former chapter house and chapel is home to Gallery II of the Diocesan Museum where visitors can admire the excellent collection of 15th-century Gothic panels and altarpieces, together with a number of sculptures and examples of medieval silverware. Highlights include Mateu Ortoneda's early 15th-century altarpiece of the Virgin in the centre of the apse, and important panels spanning the Linear Gothic to International Gothic periods.

→
Detail of the altarpiece in the apse

On the left, detail of the Annunciation

On the right, keystone on the vaulting

Present-day chapter house

The present-day chapter house is located near the chapel of Corpus Christi and reached through two ambulatories containing artworks. This is the room where the Cathedral Chapter meet when new canons take office. The entrance door is flanked inside by two polychrome carvings depicting Saint Peter the Apostle and Saint John the Baptist. They come from the altarpiece of Saint Michael that used to be on display in the cathedral and were made by the sculptor Antoni Pallàs between 1767 and 1770. The room was built in the baroque style using the familiar 17th-century layout. It has a rectangular ground plan with a groin vault divided into three sections by transverse basket arches, a moulded cornice interrupted by plaster corbels and gilded polychrome keystones carved in wood. *The Good Life* tapestry hangs on the left-hand wall. It was once owned by Archbishop Gonzalo Fernández de Heredia, and his episcopal emblem woven into the tapestry attests to this. It was bequeathed to the Cathedral Chapter in 1511. Until now the composition had been considered a figurative and symbolic compendium based on the ideas of Saint Thomas Aquinas' treatise *De regno ad Regem Cypri* concerning the principles of governing. However, recent studies point to the *Dotzè del Cristià* by the Girona-born Franciscan monk Francesc Eiximenis as the main source of inspiration for the design of the series of virtues, symbols and political ideas depicted in this valuable tapestry. A funeral pall hangs from the right-hand wall of the chamber. It was embroidered in Rome in the 17th century and donated to the Royal Monastery of Poblet by Pedro Antonio of Aragon in 1672, when the mortal remains of Alfonso V and Beatrice of Hungary were transferred there. The Cathedral Chapter purchased the tapestry in the 20th century from an antiques dealer. The donor's heraldic shield, stamped with the ducal crown and the arms of the viceroy of Naples and duke of Segorbe and Cardona, was embroidered in relief on silk with silver and gold thread of different hues. The rococo-style canons' chairs were carved in walnut in the second half of the 18th century.

The Good Life tapestry, chairs and emblem of the Chapter

The collection of tapestries

The Tarragona Cathedral Chapter has a very important collection of fifty-four tapestries that once hung in the galleries of the cloisters and inside the cathedral. The collection began to take shape in the 16th century with donations from different prelates and chapter members. Most are made with a warp of woollen or cotton thread and a weft of coloured woollen and silk thread and, sometimes, gold and silver, to create a figurative full-length image based on an original cartoon. With the exception of one tapestry woven in high warp, the rest were made with the warp in a horizontal position, or low warp, on the loom. The first tapestry in the collection was *The Good Life*, also titled *The Potestates*. It was donated by Archbishop Gonzalo Fernández de Heredia (1490-1511) and is the most valuable tapestry at the cathedral. The tapestry was woven on a high-warp loom, probably at workshops in Arras, Tournai or Brussels between 1460 and 1480. The collection expanded with two tapestries cut into uneven halves that depict *The Story of Joseph*. They were manufactured in Brussels towards the end of the 15th century and donated by Archbishop Alfonso of Aragon (1513-1514). Further additions included a fragment of an early 16th-century Flemish tapestry; and a series of tapestries left to the cathedral in the will (1575) of the prelate Gaspar Cervantes de Gaeta (1568-1575):

Detail of
The Good Life

Detail of the one of the *Samson* tapestries

the *Vegetable tapestries* (4) woven in Enghien or Oudenaarde (Flanders) in the 16th century; the *David series* (3) made towards the middle of the 16th century and attributed to the Brussels workshops; the *Tobias series* (8) from the middle of the 16th century, partly associated with other tapestries from Oudenaarde; the *Samson series* (5) from the 16th century, made by the Brussels workshops. The three sets of tapestries left in the will of Canon Diego Girón de Rebolledo (1682) form the bulk of the collection. The twenty-six tapestries were put on sale but nobody made an offer for them and the Cathedral Chapter finally decided they "were not for sale because they enhanced the beauty of the church". These tapestries are known as the *Cyrus the Great series* (8) and bear the marks of the locality and workshop; the *Allegorical series* (13) woven with woollen thread and touches of silk; the *Mystified series* (3); and the *Judith series* (2). They were all manufactured in Brussels and some of them taken from cartoons painted by Jacob Jordaens.

The collection is completed with two 16th- and 18th-century heraldic tapestries and the funeral pall from Poblet embroidered with silk, silver and gold thread in the 17th century.

The canons' old refectory

The refectory was built towards the end of the 12th century and has a pointed barrel vault. The chancel still contains part of the Roman wall built during the 1st century AD using the *opus quadratum* technique. The holes in the ashlars are proof that the wall was clad in marble, a common practice in important landmarks during the Roman Empire. Behind the arch in the wall, on the left of the chancel, we find a section of the kitchen belonging to the old refectory.

This room now houses Gallery I of the Diocesan Museum and showcases a hand-picked selection of works of art from the cathedral and other places in the archdiocese of Tarragona. Highlights include the sarcophagus of Apollo and the nine Muses (3rd century AD); the alabaster Arabic arch with traces of the original polychrome decoration from Madinat-al-Zahara, dated 960 AD, a number of tombstones (13th century), the *Deiparae*, or polychrome images of the Virgin with the Christ Child in her lap sculpted in stone (14th century), or wood (12th-14th centuries), and frescoes in the Linear Gothic style (14th century) from the long-demolished parish church of Peralta.

A tapestry depicting the story of Samson hangs above the lintel of the door leading into the room. It shows Samson destroying the Philistine temple of Dagon. It was woven in Brussels in the 17th century and is part of the cathedral's important collection of tapestries.

Doorway to the old kitchen

Tombstone inscription

Saint Thecla "La Vella"

The chapel of Saint Thecla "La Vella" (The Old) stands in the north-east end of the cathedral, separate from the great apse and in the area where the Visigothic basilica, destroyed by the Arabs in the early 8th century and rebuilt in the 10th century, is believed to have stood. It was built in the space occupied by the early cathedral —the scene of important historic events during the 11th and 12th centuries— and part of the landscaped area used as a cemetery where several bishops had been interred in the 12th and 13th centuries. Their remains are buried in the sarcophagi lining the walls of the transept by the entrance to the chapel of the Holy Sacrament.

Its austere façade features a simple door with a rounded arch and a tympanum devoid of decoration

Its austere façade features a simple door with a rounded arch and a tympanum devoid of decoration. It is framed by two stylised ornamental columns supporting two cavettos, the upper one carved in a square pattern. Above the door there is a pointed window and, on the sides, buttresses reinforced by half columns topped by capitals, with the exception of the one on the left-hand corner of the façade and the one on the eastern wall, blocked up by the building added at a later date, plus another rebuilt in the second half of the 19th century when the Chapter decided to improve the area around the cathedral. These abutments make it possible to date this chapel, along with the nearby chapel of Saint Paul, to the early part of the 13th century. Documents exist confirming that Saint Thecla "La Vella" had already been completed in 1286.

← Romanesque door

The chapel has a rectangular ground plan and is 13 metres long by 5.5 metres wide. The interior has a double ribbed vault. The wall in the chancel has two twin blind arches and a loophole that has been tiled over. Next to the north side, on the eastern wall, a funeral chapel was added a century later in 1325. It is higher, with a bell gable, arches, pointed vaults and bears the crests of its promoter Francesc Botet, whose tombstone states that he died in 1325.

Both buildings contain a noteworthy collection of tombstones and sarcophagi, including the recumbent marble effigy of an archbishop in the arcosolium on the wall of the Evangelist. When the new cathedral was built, the chapel was renamed Saint Thecla "La Vella".

Effigy of a mitred bishop

Saint Michael on the grand altarpiece

Railings in the chapel of Saint Thecla

Published by
© **Triangle Postals**

Editorial direction
Ricard Pla

Edition
Jordi Puig

Text
© **Antonio Pedro Martínez Subías**

Photography
© **Jordi Puig**

Graphic design
Joan Colomer

Layout
Vador Minobis

Translation
Mark Waudby

Printed by
Gráficas Gongraf
6-2019

Registration number: Me 556-2019

ISBN 978-84-8478-877-5

Printed in Barcelona

Triangle Postals, SL
Sant Lluís, Menorca
Tel. +34 971 15 04 51
www.triangle.cat

TRIANGLE BOOKS

CATEDRAL BASÍLICA DE TARRAGONA METROPOLITANA I PRIMADA